CLOSE CALL

Suddenly, without warning, Sarah's rope jerked, and she was yanked off her feet and dragged forward. In that split second she felt her body seize up and her mind go blank before she finally dug her ice ax in the snow and came to a stop. When her brain cleared, Sarah was afraid to sit up. Instead she looked around, stretching out her neck between her body's spasmodic shudders.

Bobby had disappeared, and Doug was on the ground too.

"Where is Bobby? What is happening?" Sarah's throat had tightened so much that she was surprised any sound came out.

How could Bobby be there one minute and gone the next? Was this some bad dream?

To the Summit

CLAIRE RUDOLF MURPHY

AN AVON  FLARE BOOK

AVON BOOKS
A division of
The Hearst Corporation
1350 Avenue of the Americas
New York, New York 10019

Copyright © 1992 by Claire Rudolf Murphy
Published by arrangement with the author
Visit our website at http://www.AvonBooks.com
Library of Congress Catalog Card Number: 91-43533
ISBN: 0-380-79537-X

First Avon Flare Printing: May 1998

AVON FLARE TRADEMARK REG. U.S. PAT. OFF. AND IN OTHER COUNTRIES, MARCA REGISTRADA, HECHO EN U.S.A.

Printed in the U.S.A.

WCD   10   9   8   7   6   5   4   3

to my parents, Fran and Kerm,
with love and gratitude

STRAPPED in the copilot's seat of a Cessna 185, seventeen-year-old Sarah Janson stared down at miles of green spruce trees broken only by twisting streams and countless small lakes. There were so many lakes that some didn't even have names. As the plane gained in elevation, Sarah's spirits rose, her body tingling as they flew over what seemed like hundreds of little mountains made of jagged black, blue, and gray rock.

Today, June 1, Sarah, her dad, and seven other climbers would begin their expedition up Mount McKinley, the tallest mountain in North America. Sarah's heart pumped with excitement, strong and ready to go. She had begged her dad for months to let her come along. Finally, here they were. She wondered if her dad, sitting right behind her, was as nervous as she.

Just then her stomach lurched, and the taste of cornflakes and milk filled Sarah's mouth. She should have ignored her dad's advice this morning at the roadhouse and eaten just a piece of toast, like she'd wanted. Sarah breathed in and out several times, slowly pushing the air out of her lungs, hoping her dad didn't notice. It wasn't too late, even now, for him to change his mind.

Thirty minutes before, standing on the airstrip in Talkeetna, Sarah had admired the beauty of The Mountain. It was sixty miles away, yet at 20,000 feet it towered far above the other mountains in the Alaska Range. Shades of orange from the morning sun lit up its peak, giving it a surreal glow. Tim Gravin, the assistant guide, had told the group last night that an orange rising sun promised fair weather. Sarah had felt so confident then, so ready to meet Tim's challenge of "to the summit." Was her body letting her down already?

Sarah rearranged her headset and then twisted her long, dark ponytail round and round with her right hand, her blue eyes focused on the terrain below. Suddenly the trees and rocks disappeared, and larger black mountains with snow emerged out of the clouds. As the plane gained even more altitude, Mount McKinley and the smaller snow-covered peaks came into view, along with glaciers upon glaciers of snow. Sarah dropped her hair and let out a sigh. It was breathtaking, even more incredible than she'd imagined. Behind her, she heard Tim and her dad moving around to get a better look.

Sarah turned and looked at Don, the pilot at the controls. Calm and sure, a slight smile around the corners of his mouth, he seemed to know no fear. Then she heard his voice talking into the microphone attached to his headset. "Isn't this something? I bring climbers up here maybe a hundred times a year, but I never get tired of this beauty."

So Don was one of those diehard Alaskans who loved everything about the state, Sarah thought. Sometimes she felt that something must be wrong with her. She couldn't deny that the scenery of Alaska was beautiful. But she didn't like Alaska, and hadn't from the minute her new stepfather, Mike, had dragged her and her mother out of Oregon to the Yup'ik Eskimo village of Mayurvik ten months ago. But whether she like Alaska or not, she was going to climb to the summit of Mount McKinley.

All winter and spring, Sarah had prepared for the expedition, never admitting to her mother and Mike how scared she was. She knew that if she displayed even the least uncertainty, her mother would refuse to let her go. Not that her mother could actually forbid her, since she spent summers with her dad, but Sarah didn't want to climb McKinley without her mother's blessing.

Sarah's stomach flipped again. This time she grabbed for the airsickness bag, as sweat broke out on her face. After almost a year in the Alaskan bush, she should have been used to small planes. Her best friend, Gretchen, back in Eugene, Oregon, told Sarah she should enjoy riding and flirting with the adventuresome bush pilots.

But not all the pilots were young and handsome, and on every plane trip Sarah got motion sickness and couldn't wait to get back onto safe ground. Yet after a few whiffs of fresh air, she always felt fine again. Was it all in her head, like her dad said?

Sarah didn't really have a choice. If she was going to live in the bush, she had to fly in small planes. With no roads to Anchorage or other villages, the only other transportation available were boats in the summertime and snow machines and dog teams in the winter. Sarah's friends in Eugene couldn't understand. "No roads

3

at all?'' they had asked in confusion during her Christmas visit.

"Well, there is one road to the airport, but that's only five miles long." They shook their heads, and Sarah gave up trying to explain.

"There it is again," Don yelled out. Sarah blinked her eyes open, trying to get her mind back on the expedition. Mayurvik was behind her, at least for now. Mount McKinley loomed into sight like a huge mound of white chocolate, towering over the other peaks. Just looking at it took Sarah's queasiness away.

Sarah and her dad had been chosen to fly the first trip into the Kahiltna Glacier base camp this morning with Tim. Doug Terell, the head guide of Summit Expeditions, had made the announcement last night before the barbeque. "We have had many father-son teams travel up Denali with us through the years, but"—Doug paused and looked at Sarah—"never have we had the privilege of guiding a father-daughter team. So, to mark this momentous occasion, the Jansons will travel on the first flight tomorrow." Everybody had whistled and clapped, especially the obnoxious college student, Bobby Snyder.

Sarah had felt her cheeks flush with embarrassment. Now she was special, marked as different, just as she had been all year in Mayurvik. What were they going to think later when they heard one-half of this special team yelling at the other half?

Sarah thought of Tim sitting behind her and felt better. All winter he had encouraged her through letters and phone calls. She remembered their first phone conversation in January when she had told him how much she loved the outdoors, how she had skied and camped for years in Oregon, and how much it meant to her to climb McKinley with her dad.

4

And then later, when she trusted him, she had said, "Tim, I'm afraid I don't have enough climbing experience. All I've climbed is Mount Hood in one day with my dad. But *please* don't say I can't come."

"Don't worry, Sarah." His voice had sounded so positive, as if he were standing with her in their house in Mayurvik, his arm around her shoulders, and looking at Mike and her mom. "A lot of techniques we use on McKinley aren't readily used on other mountains. In fact, climbing in the lower forty-eight states is completely different from climbing McKinley. We'll be taking the West Buttress route, the one 80 percent of the climbers take, and teaching you right on the mountain. Believe me, technique isn't McKinley's challenge, sitting out the weather is."

Then Tim had paused for a long time, and Sarah had wondered if the connection was lost. But soon his voice had jumped back over the wire. "Sarah, very few seventeen-year-olds can handle climbing Denali. They just aren't strong enough mentally or physically. But based on your outdoor experience and your running background, we think you can do it. Remember—the hardest part will be the mental challenge, not the physical."

Sarah had gripped the phone and nodded. "I learned that from running, Tim. I really think I can do it, but everybody seems to think I'm crazy. Am I?"

"Listen to me, Sarah. We have a summit guide with us now who is twenty-seven and has led several climbs over the past three years. I told her about you. She said she wanted to climb Denali at seventeen and is sure she could have done it. But she lived in Colorado, and it took her seven more years to come up with the money."

That night Sarah had believed that, with Tim at her side, she could make the summit, especially after she heard that, between them, Tim and Doug had climbed

McKinley fifteen times. Gabe Moses, the apprentice guide, had never climbed McKinley, but he had extensive climbing experience.

Sarah tried to bring back that confidence now. As they flew high above the Kahiltna Glacier, it looked like an undisturbed carpet of snow. But as the plane descended and flew right over it, Sarah realized that the surface actually consisted of thousands of ridges of rocks and blue-green holes up to several hundred feet deep.

"Those are crevasses," Tim yelled out.

Her dad let out a low whistle. Sarah had heard a lot about crevasses. Tim, Doug, and Gabe had made sure of that yesterday when the whole group had practiced crevasse rescues. "Folks, our very lives depend on knowing these safety skills and having confidence in one another," Doug had said, staring at each one.

Two teachers from Anchorage, Wendy Benson and Laura Marsh, had helped Sarah relax. Wendy, short and powerfully built with a mass of dark, curly hair, had kept Sarah distracted with her nonstop talk. And Sarah had enjoyed the company of the quieter Laura even more, admiring her long legs and calm smile.

Yesterday morning had been spent in the Summit log pavilion assembling and checking over their gear, making sure it fit and worked properly.

In the afternoon, the guides fixed a line in the rafters of the pavilion. All nine of them practiced repelling, sliding down the rope with their harnesses on, into a mock crevasse area and then pulling themselves out with the jumar ascenders on the rope. It was surprisingly hard work, especially when Doug made them try it a second time with a loaded pack on their back. Tim helped Sarah work as quickly as possible getting in and out of her harnesses, tying knots, clipping into the rope,

6

and using the ascenders on the fixed line. Finally, by dinner, she felt more sure of herself.

She could thank Sam Donnelly for that. After the hours of practice, the fun-loving furniture store owner from Denver had started singing, "Rope 'em in, little doggies," and got the whole group laughing, even her dad and Doug.

When she had met Sam two days ago, she had liked him immediately. With his short, overweight body, he looked like the Pillsbury Doughboy. Here was somebody who might not be as physically tough as some of the others, but he didn't seem to let it worry him.

Sarah had enjoyed the hard work and companionship of the day until Bobby Snyder sat down next to her at the barbeque. "Better have two mooseburgers. You're going to need them, to carry your share of the weight." Sarah had been worried about the possible sexist remarks. Here it comes, she thought.

"Rumor has it this is the last good meal we're going to get for a month," Bobby continued.

Sarah nodded, but didn't look up, fiddling with the pickle on her plate.

"I hear you used to live in Oregon."

She wanted to shout, "Yes, but I want to live in Oregon *now*."

"The University of Alaska's just not that sophisticated, know what I mean? So I've thought about going Outside to school. But the out-of-state tuition, whew . . ." Bobby took another bite of his burger. "What's it like in Eugene? Does it really rain as much as they say?"

Sarah stood up, as if she were heading back to the food line. "It's the greatest place in the world." She made a detour around the table, where she dropped her plate in the trash can. Then she headed toward the hangar.

Suddenly Don pulled back the plane's throttle to land. A faint odor of oil and gas filled the plane. Sarah kept staring at the white ground coming up at them. She knew that if she closed her eyes, she would feel even dizzier. Trying to distract herself, she watched Don adjust the throttle and gentle the engine. In the quieter plane, she could hear the wind rushing by.

Then her head almost hit the ceiling as the Cessna bumped the ground with a series of jolts. Finally, the skis found the glacier surface, the tail dropped, and the plane came to a halt. With the pilot's help, Sarah hurriedly opened the door and hopped out into a frozen world of sun and snow. Here she was in winter, only forty-five minutes away from the seventy-degree weather in Talkeetna. Layered in clothes and dressed for thirty-degree weather on the glacier, Sarah didn't realize how hot she'd been until she got off the plane.

Unloading their gear took only a few minutes and, before Sarah even had a chance to look around, Don was taxiing down the snow-packed runway. With a thumbs-up sign for good luck, he took to the air. Sarah waved good-bye to the red bird. Just then, her insulated sleeping pad went flying up the glacier, pushed by the heavy gust of wind from the plane. Sarah sprinted up in its path, trying to retrieve it.

"Stop! Stop, Sarah! Don't take another step." She stopped, frozen in her tracks, startled at Tim's commanding voice.

"But it's the only sleeping pad I brought."

"Let it go." Tim walked carefully over to Sarah, poking the ground with a ski pole as he moved along. "Remember all those crevasses we saw from the air?

Remember all our work yesterday? You could have stepped into one and been killed. It's pretty well trampled down here and generally safe. But you didn't know that. Remember—we told you, never, ever, walk around without being roped in, unless we've made a crevasse check first. You can never be too safe."

Tim roped in and continued checking the area, while Sarah stood there shaking. Then her dad spoke. "Sarah, what were you thinking? I didn't spend all this money to have you disappear down a hole while chasing a silly pad!"

Fighting back tears, Sarah said nothing, wondering why she had thought this trip would change things between her and her dad. Her body felt so tired.

She wished she could go down a hole, if just for a while. Time unroped and called out that the area was safe. Sarah forced herself to follow her dad over to Tim. "Well, you two, we get the fun job of unpacking the goods here." Handing Sarah a box, Tim softened his voice and said, "I know I yelled at you, but it's so important to be thinking every moment you're on this mountain. One careless mistake and it's all over."

"But what about my pad?"

"No problem. I've already radioed back to Talkeetna to have them send another one with the next planeload."

Sarah's dad looked at her as if to say, "There goes some more money."

The three of them walked around the glacier, finally picking out a campsite somewhat away from the other expeditions. Sarah was amazed at how many climbers were on the glacier. Forty or fifty yellow tents dotted the snow.

As they carried goods and equipment to their site, Sarah began to relax. She looked up at the blue sky and then down at the glistening snow. How can I be upset on such a perfect day in such a perfect place? she wondered.

Tim instructed Sarah and her dad to move the extra supplies over to the spot where they would build a cache. A wave of panic came over Sarah. She'd forgotten that they'd brought along the extra supplies needed to keep them going for a week, in case they were weathered in. It was sunny now, but she knew that the fog could roll into the camp at any time and the planes might not be able to fly.

What would she do for days on this glacier with only her dad to yell at her and Tim, who had suddenly turned into a dictator? She had come to climb the mountain, not wait around.

The second planeload buzzed overhead, and Sarah breathed easier. Walking over to the landing area, she waved frantically, hoping Sam or Laura would look down and see her. As Sam climbed out of the plane, Sarah smiled. She could use a little music right now.

Bounding off the plane, Bobby waltzed over and put his arm around her. "Well, sweetheart, looks pretty good." Sarah smiled and moved away.

Doug stretched out his arms to the sky and yelled, "Is this weather great or what?" Then he clapped his hands and said, "Well, let's get this airplane unloaded so Don here can bring back the final three."

After unloading the plane, they waved Don off, and then Doug directed Bobby, Tim, and Sarah's dad to move the supplies over to the campsite. "Sarah and Sam, I'll put you on the cache-building crew."

A few minutes later, as she and Sam shoveled snow on top of the cache of emergency supplies, Sarah surprised herself by saying, "Sam, sing us a song."

"Sure." But first he leaned his heavy body over and

whispered to Sarah, "What's going on here? Awfully solemn for our first day on the glacier." Sarah shrugged her shoulders.

"Come on. Your father's scowling and you're acting like a whipped puppy dog." Finally, Sarah gave in and told him about the sleeping pad incident.

"Hey, don't let it get to you. Everybody makes mistakes. If I'd been here, it probably would have happened to me instead. I'm the one they're all worried about, you know."

"But I'm the young one, and a girl at that."

"Hey, you wouldn't be here if they didn't think you could do it. That's what I keep telling myself. If I let myself get negative, I know I'll never make it."

chapter 2

WHEN the last planeload landed, Sarah and Sam arrived just in time to hear Wendy climb out and say, "Wow! This is incredible." Sarah stopped and looked around again. It is incredible, she thought. I am lucky to be here. Who cares how my dad acts? I've got to make the most of it.

Kahiltna Glacier was ideally situated—a flat bowl area between jutting mountains on either side—and a perfect camping spot. By now the sun had warmed up the glacier, and all around climbers from other expeditions were out sunning, eating, socializing. One climber was even juggling, and another was playing the violin. It was like one big party, but Sarah didn't want to party. She wanted to climb.

Already at 7,200 feet the effects of altitude could be felt. It was harder to breathe up here, Sarah thought, but then she smiled. She'd heard for years about the positive effects of training in a higher altitude, then

12

racing at a lower altitude. Maybe this trip really would help her running.

With everyone finally present, Doug spoke to the team. He put his arms around Wendy and Laura, then turned and looked up at the mountain. "Well, gang, our task is simple. All we have to do is climb Denali." Sarah laughed with the others. Simple—she'd have to remember that.

After they unloaded the plane, Don shook hands all around, finally ending with Sarah. He grabbed her right hand and squeezed it between both of his large, muscular ones. "Good luck, kid. Wish I could be there when you make the summit." Sarah's eyes glistened, but she didn't know what to say, so she just squeezed his hand even harder.

Climbing into the plane, he turned and waved, calling out, "Make it up there quick, you hear? I haven't got all summer."

As Don revved up the engine, Sarah's heart began beating faster. This was it. Her last chance to back out. Her first chance to start climbing.

Then, while Don taxied down the snowy airstrip, Sarah's heart almost thumped out of her chest as she watched Wendy sprinting after the plane, waving frantically.

"Wendy, STOP, WEN-DY! For God's sake, stop. What the hell are you doing?" Doug yelled out. Wendy stopped in her tracks and whirled around.

"I . . . I . . ."

From where she stood, Sarah could see Wendy's whole body shaking and her face turn gray, as though she was about to faint.

"You could have killed yourself and the trip has barely begun. Are you roped in? Have you checked for crevasses?'' Wendy shook her head. Everyone else was deathly quiet.

"There was a woman climber who died up here in 1976 on her first day's climb up Kahiltna Glacier. She had unroped to go to the latrine and slipped down a long, hidden crack into a crevasse. Buried in hundreds of feet of snow with no rope—there was absolutely no chance for a rescue.''

Sarah started shivering, a cold spot growing in her heart and moving up into her throat.

"What did we tell you yesterday in Talkeetna?'' Doug went on. "Never walk around unroped unless the area's been checked for crevasses.''

Sarah was on her guard. She'd been here for three hours now and had more than learned her lesson from the sleeping pad episode. But Wendy had just stepped off the airplane.

"I thought since everyone else was unroped and they'd been here for a while . . .'' Wendy's voice trailed off. "I was just so excited to be here and to send Don off.'' Wendy looked down at the snow and then back up. "It was a foolish mistake and it won't happen again.'' Sarah thought she heard Wendy's voice crack.

"It better not.'' Pointing to the mountain, Doug said, "You won't have a second chance. It's not that friendly.'' He pierced the ground with a ski pole, then continued, "You've got to be thinking every minute you're up here. Anything can go wrong. Your very life and the lives of all of us depend on each individual thinking and working as a team member. You can walk back over here, Wendy. It has been checked for crevasses, but you didn't know that. Besides, when is an airstrip with a live plane on it ever safe?''

Doug took his eyes off Wendy as she walked back over, and stared at the group. "And as long as we're on the subject of safety, don't forget about yesterday's lesson on avalanches. They're not a problem here on the Kahiltna Glacier because it's so wide. But look way over there and up at the mountains. When we hit eleven to twelve thousand feet, that's when we enter avalanche territory. When we do . . ." Doug stopped again and pointed at each climber in turn as he punctuated his words. "Stay away from walls, cliffs, and overhangs, and never, I mean *never,* put packs near any of them. You've got to stay out in the wide open spaces, and that can get tricky in the small campsites higher up. That snow can come down so fast, burying you or your gear with it like that." Doug managed to snap his fingers in spite of his gloves.

He took in a deep breath and slowly let it out, lowering his voice when he finally spoke again. "Tim, Gabe, and I refuse to take a group up the mountain that doesn't follow the safety rules. Stay roped in, stay away from ledges, and most of all, stay alert." With a big sweep of his hand, he said, "Welcome to Denali."

Sarah breathed slowly in and out, closing her eyes and thinking about all that Doug had said. Was she ready to concentrate and stop thinking about her personal problems all the time? She'd better be. When she opened her eyes, Doug was smiling, a new man again.

"Okay, let's get on with it. How 'bout we move the final load over to our campsite? We'll set aside the supplies and equipment for tomorrow's carry and build another cache for the supplies that we'll carry on the second day. Then we ought to be ready for some lunch."

Doug walked over to Wendy and put his arm around her, looking up so that everyone could hear. "Tim has marked the danger areas with the double wands wrapped in orange tape. Stay away from those danger

15

areas, and if you venture out farther than this main area, rope in.'' Wendy and the rest of the group nodded.

As Doug walked away, Sarah remembered that long ago the Athabaskan Indians had named the mountain Denali, ''the High One.'' They believed the mountain had a power all its own. Doug believed it and now Sarah was beginning to believe it too. The mountain was beautiful, but it could kill you.

Over the years more than forty climbers had been killed on McKinley. Last night, Doug said Summit Expeditions had never lost a climber on one of their trips. Today, he demonstrated he was determined to keep it that way.

As Sarah carried another load of packs over to the campsite, she realized how much the glacier had warmed up since she'd first arrived this morning. With all this work, she was beginning to sweat. She unzipped her royal blue polar fleece jacket and took it off, along with her navy polypropylene shirt, and worked in her T-shirt.

This morning she hadn't even needed her green down coat with the fur ruff or the electric-blue-and-green-striped Gore-Tex windbreaker her dad had just bought her the other day in Anchorage. He'd let Sarah pick out the entire matching outfit, even including supergaiters to fit over the tops of her climbing boots and up her legs to her knees.

For now, she padded around the campsite in the sealskin mukluks Mike had asked Jack Tommy's mother to make for her last Christmas. Sarah loved the soft feel of the sealskin, and how warm the mukluks had kept her feet as she walked to school every morning last winter. The day she went to Jack's house for the fitting was the first time she had actually talked to him outside of class.

Jack. She was surprised when he had asked her to the prom—and was even more so when she had a good time. He'd looked so handsome that night with his short haircut and new suit for college.

Walking alongside Gabe, Sarah noticed that the Yup'ik Eskimo guide was also wearing mukluks. "Gabe, are you going to wear your mukluks with your snowshoes?"

"I don't think so," he said, smiling. "The double-plastic climbing boots grip better. But I'll wear the mukluks in camp. I see you have some too." Sarah nodded. Maybe sometime she'd talk to him about Mayurvik.

Later as they built the cache together, Sarah said, "I really like my mukluks."

Gabe nodded. "In Yup'ik mukluk means, 'I'm wearing spirits on my feet.' "

"Well," said Sarah, laughing, "that's good. I need all the help I can get."

Doug called the group together and demonstrated how to mark both caches. "Just remember how critical it is to have this emergency cache available. If we get weathered in or someone gets hurt or sick, we could be stranded here for a long time. This food would save us. Look around at the other double-wand markings. Those are caches from other expeditions on the mountain."

Sam motioned Sarah over to a nearby marker. "Take a look at this. 'Johnson expedition—May 12th—West Buttress route.' These guys should be coming down pretty soon." Sam seemed to be breathing hard, but suddenly he burst out singing, "We've only just begun . . ." Sarah laughed. His voice wasn't that good, but Sam didn't seem to be embarrassed about it or worried about saving his strength, either. Yesterday when he was the slowest in practice, he just kept smiling and

17

whistling, even when Bobby talked about how hungry he was for dinner.

"Lunchtime," Tim announced. Sarah sat down and stretched out her legs. She realized how hungry she was as she ate the dried meat and cheese with crackers. Six o'clock this morning seemed like a long time ago.

Looking around the circle, Sarah noticed Wendy chatting away with Sam. It would take Sarah hours, days, even weeks to get over her fear and embarrassment about the airstrip episode. Although Doug had publicly embarrassed Wendy, she seemed to have put the whole thing behind her, whereas Sarah was still reprimanding herself for the sleeping pad episode. Thank goodness only Tim and her dad were around for that. And it appeared they hadn't said a word to anyone else about it.

Sarah turned to Tim, who was sitting beside her. "Tim, is the mountain called McKinley or Denali?"

"It goes by both names. But most climbers and Alaskans prefer the Indian name Denali. It only got the name McKinley because some prospector in 1896 didn't know it already had a name, so he named it after William McKinley, the Republican presidential candidate at the time." He shook his head. "But don't you think Denali describes its true nature better than McKinley, a lackluster American president who never even saw the mountain?"

Sarah nodded. Denali it would be. She looked around, realizing everyone had stopped talking to hear Tim's explanation. Munching on an apple, she watched as Wendy's eyes moved to the airstrip, staring at it for a long time. Enjoying the crisp texture of the apple, Sarah kept looking at Wendy. Maybe she hadn't recovered as quickly as it first appeared.

Doug stood up on a camp stool. "Okay, gang. Time

to set up camp. After that, we'll get out the equipment and practice roping in and working with our snowshoes and sleds. Hopefully all this will only take a couple of hours and then you can spend the rest of the afternoon relaxing, enjoying the sunshine, and socializing with other climbers. As you may have gathered, this is a very friendly place."

Since they'd already done a lot of work, the camp setup went quickly. Tim and Gabe finished organizing the kitchen area. Doug, Bobby, Sam, and Sarah's dad built tent platforms. Sarah, Laura, and Wendy boiled water for the rest of today and tomorrow's trek.

Sarah watched with admiration as Wendy worked the stove. Wendy smiled. "I know Doug said only the guides would be working the stoves, but I think the big boss relented today because I've worked with these kinds of stoves before, and since my colossal mistake today, he also knew I needed some bucking up."

"You'd just gotten off the plane, for Pete's sake. Doug expects us to be perfect," Sarah said, scooping snow into the pot. "I did the same thing before you got here."

"You did?" Wendy looked up, startled.

"Sure. I wasn't roped in, and I chased after my sleeping pad. Tim and my dad really yelled at me."

As the stove perked along, Wendy put her arm around Sarah's shoulders. "Well, we're both lucky it was nothing worse. I'd rather learn my lesson now than later on when it could really be serious."

Sarah shivered, then said to herself, "No negative thoughts."

chapter 3

IT took a long time to boil all the water, four quarts a day per person, and by that time Sarah's dad and Sam had already set up the tent and the others were working with their gear.

Sarah quickly changed into her climbing boots and then tried on her snowshoes. Adjusting the straps, she looked over just in time to see Bobby fall on his backside. Wendy winked at her and Sarah barely stifled a laugh in time. But then as she slid along the crunchy snow, she slipped, too, and so did most everybody else.

When Sarah finally felt comfortable with the snowshoes, she loaded some packs into her sled. Then she clipped the waistband of the sled harness around her waist and tried walking around. Some sleds could carry up to 100 pounds. On the daily climbs, Sarah would be pulling around twenty-five pounds in the sled and carrying forty pounds of gear in her pack.

Sarah's dad came snowshoeing over. "How you

doing? Got those snowshoes on correctly? It looks like you've got the sled loaded down too much. I don't want you getting too tired the first day's climb.''

"Dad, I'm fine," Sarah said, moving away. Why couldn't he ever trust her to know what she was doing? Why had he brought her on this trip if all he was going to do was babysit?

When her dad left, Sarah tried on her backpack. Hefting the forty-pound pack onto her back, she struggled to adjust the weight. Last winter she had spent hours poring over catalogs, searching for the perfect pack, but she couldn't decide. Finally, in frustration she had called her dad. "Dad, how am I supposed to find the right backpack through a catalog."

"Listen, Sarah, if you can't decide, then just wait, and we'll buy one in Anchorage."

"Oh, that's great. All the literature says how important the backpack is and, if it doesn't fit correctly, your back could be sore for the entire trip. I've got to practice so I feel comfortable with it. And now time is running out."

"I'm sorry, honey, but so is mine. I've got a sales meeting right now. I'll call you later."

At the girls' class A state basketball tournament in Anchorage in March, Sarah's mom and Mike took her shopping. It was the first time they acknowledged that she was going on the expedition. The pack was perfect—bright red, standing against the wall at the sporting goods store beckoning, "Buy me." A soft pack with an internal frame, it snuggled against Sarah's shoulders comfortably.

The salesperson had put it aside for her, and she bought it the day after Mayurvik lost the championship game. Sarah had scored fifteen points with ten assists, but it wasn't enough. She knew she didn't care about winning as much as some of the other girls, which only alienated her from them more.

Sarah had come back to Mayurvik and spent the next few weeks skiing and then hiking when the snow melted. Every afternoon on the tundra above the village, she practiced carrying her new pack, loaded down with forty pounds of flour. At first, she thought she would collapse under the weight, but it grew easier as the days grew longer. Right now, though, it felt heavier than ever.

"As you put on your packs, just remember this, guys"—Tim's voice was so much more soothing than Doug's—"if we weren't ferrying our supplies expedition style, we'd each be carrying fifty to one hundred pounds on our backs the first few days." The group groaned in unison.

"We're in no hurry to go helter-skelter up the mountain alpine style, like some of the more experienced hotshot climbers. By ferrying the supplies back and forth we can take it slower, get used to the terrain, climate, and altitude, and enjoy ourselves a little more. So don't forget that when your pack feels heavy tomorrow."

Sarah took off her pack and sat down on it, resting for a few moments before attacking the harnesses. Bobby came cruising by with his harnesses already on, and said, "Tired already, sweetheart?"

Laura called over as she struggled into her harnesses, "Funny thing. I didn't know it was Valentine's Day." Sarah could have hugged her.

Sarah stood up and picked up her harnesses. It was quite a project getting into them, but she knew that more than anything else they would ensure her safety on the mountain. The seat or waist harness fit around her behind and cinched around her waist in front with a carabiner. Through the large metal loop of the carabiner a rope was pulled that would tie Sarah to the other two climbers on her rope team.

Sarah slipped one arm, then the other into the chest harness, which fit around her shoulders, and then fastened it with another carabiner. Yesterday she had learned that the chest harness would help prevent her from flipping upside down if she fell into a crevasse. She tied the climbing rope into both carabiners.

Sarah roped in with Wendy and Laura, and they took a long trek around the glacier. After a while Sarah seemed to get the rhythm and was feeling more comfortable by the time they met an expedition of Japanese women. Wendy excitedly asked them if they were heading up or down the mountain, but the women only smiled and bowed. The more Wendy asked them, the more they smiled and nodded, then continued on their way.

When Sarah, Wendy, and Laura stopped for a water break, Sarah said, "Well, I can't decide if they looked tired enough to have made the summit."

"I know. I wish we could just sit down and talk to them. There are so few women on this mountain. Well," Wendy said, pulling her shoulders back, "next on the improvement plan—learn Japanese." She laughed.

"It does look like the United Nations around here," Laura said, taking another long sip of water.

"Yeah," Sarah said, stretching her neck out. "Didn't Tim say that thirty-three percent of Denali climbers were from other countries?"

"Then the rest must be white, middle-aged men," Wendy said, and all three women laughed. "Well, let's move along. I'm ready for some relaxation."

When Sarah got back to camp, her dad waved her

over to another campsite, where he introduced her to some climbers from Seattle. They all talked about the beauty of the Pacific Northwest. It made Sarah homesick, until she was distracted by a group of handicapped climbers who joined them. Except for their three guides, all six of the climbers had artificial limbs. Sarah tried to imagine what it would be like to climb with such a disability, until she realized that the group was silently looking at her.

Her dad tapped her arm. "Sarah, Alex here asked how old you were."

"Oh, I'm sorry. Daydreaming about the summit, I guess." Everybody smiled. "I'm seventeen."

"Seventeen," several murmured, and then Alex said, "Wow, that's impressive. You must be some athlete."

The handicapped climbers started talking to her excitedly as if they shared something in common, as if they were all breaking new ground. Sarah's dad was smiling at the attention, but Sarah hadn't really thought about being unusual, and now it was making her nervous. She just wanted to climb Denali for herself, and for her dad, too, she had to admit. Her mother would love her no matter what. But she didn't want a lot of attention—at least not until she had really done it.

Later, over the dinner of beef Stroganoff, everybody was in fine spirits, especially Doug. "Gang, I know you've had a great time socializing today, but get some sleep, too, because we want to get cracking tomorrow before the sun gets too high, melting our glorious snow and slowing us down.

"Our first carry will be up to Camp 1 at 7,700. That's five miles and should take about two hours one way, weather permitting. Then we'll climb back here to sleep and the next day back up to 7–7 with our second load. It's gonna be great." Doug went around patting people

24

on the back. "Hey, guys, every expedition needs a name. What will ours be?"

Suddenly the group was quiet. Sarah tried desperately to think of something, but her mind was blank. "June bugs," Wendy called out and everybody laughed.

"That's us," Bobby said, "flitting up the mountain."

Flitting or not, Sarah could hardly wait to get started. She'd been patient all day, but now, lying in her bag, she couldn't get to sleep. She turned to look at her dad's peaceful face, his dark, graying hair squished on his down coat. Why can't we just let each other be? she wondered.

Even Sam's steady snoring couldn't relax her anxious body. Could it be only last night that she'd slept in the Summit Expeditions pavilion—the Talkeetna Hilton, as Doug called it? Snuggled deep in her new Poly-Fil sleeping bag and surrounded by ice picks, bunny boots, harnesses, and crampons, Sarah couldn't sleep last night either—not after finally meeting the people she would spend the next three weeks with, twenty-four hours a day.

All winter Sarah could hardly believe she was really going to climb Denali, and now here she was. No one in Mayurvik could believe it, either. Just one more thing that made her different from the Yup'ik culture.

In the beginning the villagers had tried to be friendly. Some of the elders had invited her to learn how to Eskimo dance for the potlatch celebration. But after a few practices, she realized that her hips swayed too much, just like a Kass'aq, and she stopped going. She was fascinated by the stories behind their dances, and by the way the elders danced in winter to relieve the tensions and chase away the spirits. But she was not part of them.

"Kass'aq" or gussuk was one of the few Yup'ik

words she had learned. She was called it from the beginning, and didn't feel that it was a negative or a positive word. It just said what she was—a white girl. Later she learned that it came from the Russian word *cossack*—the cossacks had been the first white men to visit western Alaska.

When she wrote Gretchen about her loneliness in Mayurvik and her possible expedition up McKinley, even Gretchen didn't understand. "You amaze me. I could never climb a mountain, let alone the tallest one in North America. Gymnastics is scary enough for me. But living in the bush this year has made you tough."

Right. Tough. Sarah didn't feel tough at all. What she really wanted was her old life in Eugene—running races at Hayward Field, watching Gretchen's gymnastic meets, walking in the rain.

Her dad's solution to unhappiness was action and adventure. Don't talk about it, do it. Last summer, while visiting him for a month, Sarah sensed he wasn't very happy with his new sales job on the road. He threw himself into her training for the San Francisco marathon. He coached her every day, sure she was going to set a national record for sixteen-year-old girls. Then, when she had to drop out at twenty-two miles, he acted as though it had been Sarah's idea to run in the first place—and a wrong one at that. They never talked about it after that, but Sarah knew she had bitterly disappointed her dad.

During her Christmas break with him in San Francisco, they watched a *National Geographic* special on television about mountain climbing. At the end of the program, Sarah could still remember the commentator saying, "Most of the world's tallest mountains demand years of experience before a climber is ready to attempt their summit. But the West Buttress route of Mount

McKinley is different. Thousands of accomplished ath-
letes have reached the summit with a guided expedition
company, *if* they were in top physical condition when
they started the climb. Perhaps that explains the great
appeal McKinley has for so many people."

A few days later her dad casually mentioned he was
thinking of climbing Mount McKinley the following
June. Sarah immediately said, "Dad, I want to climb
McKinley with you."

"What, are you out of your mind? A sixteen-year-
old on that mountain? There's no way they'd let you
go, and I'm not going to be responsible to your mother
if something happens. She still hasn't forgiven me for
the marathon."

"But I'll be seventeen in March," Sarah said, standing in his living room. "And you heard what they said
on the program. I dare you to find another seventeen-
year-old in this country who's in better shape."

"But it's not just a physical challenge. It's a head trip
too. What about the marathon when you dropped out?"

"You made me drop out."

"I never wanted you to run it in the first place. Nobody that young should be running marathons. You
could have ruined your running career because of it."
Her dad got up and went into the kitchen. "Your high
school coach was furious. You've got to take directions
on the expedition, you know, and work together as a
team."

"Something we haven't done since you two got divorced." Guilt. It always got to him.

"Sarah, we got divorced four years ago. Your mother's happy, and you and I are still a team."

"I'm not happy in Mayurvik. Are you happy here?"
Sarah said, looking around his sparse apartment. "Why
can't I live with you?"

"You see how I live, on the road all the time."

"Do you still think I can be a great college runner like you?"

"Good. I was only good," her dad said, slamming a jar on the counter. "Of course you can. You can do anything you set your mind to."

"Then I want to climb McKinley." Her dad looked at her and grinned.

"And Dad, how can I possibly turn into a collegiate runner living in Mayurvik?"

"I think the time in Mayurvik has been helpful for you. It's given you a chance to slow down and stop racing so much. You've also had a chance to reevaluate things."

"I'm tough, you know," Sarah said, punching the cushion on a kitchen chair. "Nobody could have a dad like you and not be tough." Sarah could feel her voice breaking. But crying never worked with her dad. She tightened her voice and tried to make it sound hard. "And if I don't go, it'll mean another month we won't be together."

"Okay, okay. You can climb McKinley with me, *if*— and that's a very big if—the expedition company gives their approval. But your mother is going to kill me."

Flying back to Alaska, Sarah felt so happy inside, for the first time since she'd moved to Alaska. Saying good-bye wasn't so hard that time because she and her dad were going to do something together, just the two of them. Her mother had said Sarah had to give Mayurvik a year and then maybe they could work something out with her dad for her senior year. Climbing McKinley would prove to her dad how self-reliant she could be.

On that clear January afternoon, as she flew out of Anchorage en route to Mayurvik, Sarah saw McKinley, huge and white and beautiful, jutting through the clouds, as if calling her to the summit. It was an omen. She would return.

Later her dad was thrilled to find out they would be Summit Expeditions' first father-daughter team, and his pride won out. He started calling Sarah more often, giving her suggestions for training and discussing equipment. They finally had something to talk about other than her schoolwork, since her dad never wanted to talk about feelings. At last they had a new connection after their old one had been shattered when she dropped out of the marathon.

Tonight, on the mountain, awake and restless, Sarah thought, I will not drop out of this race too.

chapter 4

SUNLIGHT flooded through the bright yellow expedition tent when Sarah woke up the next morning, Day 2. She rolled over in her sleeping bag, and kicked her legs around to warm herself up.

Where was she? The ceiling and walls began to close in around her and grow fuzzy. She tried to focus. Closing her eyes, she breathed slowly in and out. Finally, her mind cleared and she sat up. Denali—Kahiltna base camp—7,200 feet above sea level and her dad still asleep. How could he sleep? She looked around. Sam was sleeping too. She'd forgotten he was in their tent. With only three tents on the trip, Sarah was relieved Sam was their partner for now and not Bobby.

Shivering, Sarah started to crawl back into her warm sleeping bag, but then she stopped herself. No, she was going to beat her dad and Sam to breakfast. Digging down to the bottom of the bag, she pulled out her clothes quietly, so as not to wake them.

30

Sarah hated dressing in a tent. The dome tent was perfect for surviving the weather on Denali, but its low ceiling made it impossible to stand up. Wriggling around on the floor, she managed to get dressed.

First, she pulled on her polypropylene long underwear. Then she sat up and put on her three layers of socks—a nylon inner sock, a coated nylon vapor-barrier sock, and finally a heavy wool sock. These feet were not going to get cold, though she had argued with her dad about the need for all these items. Next her polar fleece jacket and bottoms, followed by her wind coat and pants. Then she put on her climbing boots and grabbed her down coat in case it was really cold.

Crawling out of the tent, Sarah took in the silent white landscape dotted with orange and yellow tents. No trees, no vegetation—just sunlight making patterns on the snow. Doug, Tim, and Gabe were already up cooking breakfast.

Sarah stretched her arms to the sky and yawned. She felt so good. It looked like a perfect climbing day.

"Good morning, Sarah." Tim waved her over. "First one up makes coffee."

Sarah hated coffee and could never understand her mother's devotion to it, but this morning nothing sounded better.

"How'd you sleep?" Doug asked as he opened a food bag and handed Sarah the coffee.

"Terrific. At first I was too excited to sleep, but finally my tired body won out."

As the other climbers trickled out, Sarah and Gabe fixed a breakfast of dehydrated eggs. Sarah was so hungry even this sick, powdery concoction looked appealing. As they stirred the eggs, Doug went into a long story about his life with Summit Expeditions and his dream of climbing Everest. At least with Doug around, you were guaranteed not to have to talk about yourself.

Sarah waved to her dad as he came out of their tent, but he pretended not to see her. Maybe he was disappointed that she was already up. Sarah couldn't, wouldn't, let herself worry about it.

"Let's get ready to go, folks," Doug said after a few minutes. "Time's a wasting." Sarah loaded up her gear, trying to move quickly but not rush and make a mistake, either. Getting into the harnesses was easier today.

"Let's see," Doug directed. "Sam and Laura will be on the lead team with me, followed by Tim's team of Wendy and Bobby. Gabe's team of Sarah and John will bring up the rear."

As Sarah roped in behind Gabe, she felt safe. Even though Gabe had never climbed Denali, he had been climbing all around Alaska for over six years.

"Okay, gang, Heartbreak Hill will be coming right up with a downhill of over three hundred feet." Sarah could see the excitement in Doug's eyes. How many times had he done this and yet he still couldn't wait to get started. "Going downhill with a sled can be a problem. Make sure you keep your rope taut between you and the guy ahead of you, so you don't go crashing into him and push both of you into a crevasse." The big *C* word again, Sarah thought. "Just move at a steady pace; don't get going too fast, and you'll be fine."

The sun continued to shine brightly in the blue sky as Sarah's team followed the others snowshoeing down the hill. Sarah loved how open and full of light the glacier was.

"God, this would have made one hell of a beautiful downhill ski run," Bobby yelled out. Sarah was relieved they weren't skiing. She'd tried skiing with a pack last year at Mount Bachelor and fell many times. The pack had made her top-heavy and unbalanced. At least with snowshoes on she felt steadier.

"It sure would have," called out Tim. "But look at all those hidden crevasses under Mount Francis way over there." The ropes were 150 feet long, with 50 feet between each climber, but on a clear day like today Sarah could hear Tim perfectly.

Farther ahead, Gabe pointed up to a large crack that could hardly be seen until they were almost on top of it. Cut into the snow was a wide, dark hole that dropped down almost three hundred feet.

Sarah felt around to make sure her chest harness was secure, then moved closer to take a look. "Big enough for a train to get lost in," Sam said as Gabe whistled. Sarah stared, her blood frozen.

Moving away from the crevasse, Doug stopped the group for a water break. Wendy pulled up alongside Sarah and whispered, "I have no idea how I'm going to drink four quarts of water a day. I hate drinking water."

"I know what you mean." And yet Sarah found she was thirsty.

"Congratulations! You've just completed your first mile." Sarah stared at Tim to make sure he wasn't making fun of them, then took a long sip of water and admired the scenery. She felt terrific and even managed to give her dad a smile.

Right before they started up again, Doug called out, "Look to your right. We're about to turn north up the main Kahiltna Glacier. We don't want to get too close to those to those nasty crevasses around Mount Francis's base, so we'll take the longer western route to avoid them."

"Going east looks shorter and safe enough. Why not

33

take it?'' Bobby called out. Sarah wished he would zip his mouth.

"Guess you weren't listening, Bobby," Tim called back. "Hundreds of crevasses. But be my guest. Untie yourself and we'll see who gets to 7,700 camp first.''

Bobby straightened his wraparound glacier glasses and smiled. "Hey, don't get so serious, Tim. Think I'd want to desert this group of happy campers?'' Laura looked over at Sarah and raised her eyebrows.

With Bobby quieted for a time, Sarah enjoyed the silence and the rhythmic sound of snowshoes crunching the snow. Her snowshoes were gripping the snow well, her feet comfortably warm. From up ahead Sam's whistling came drifting back, a much gentler song than usual. Sarah wondered what it was until she heard Wendy ask him at the next water stop.

"Sam, what have you been whistling?"

" 'Edelweiss' from *The Sound of Music*. You know, the song about the delicate white flower."

"It's beautiful, Sam," Sarah said, surprised to hear her own voice.

Sam kept whistling, and as Sarah started climbing again, she pretended she was Maria von Trapp running through the Swiss Alps and later doing everything in her power to escape from the Nazis with the man and the children she loved. Once, a couple of years ago, she had watched the movie on late-night TV with Gretchen, and they had both cried.

All around her everything was white, like the edelweiss flower. But there were no green meadows. Not a speck of color anywhere, except pieces of litter—a raisin box, Hershey bar wrapper, plastic sandwich bag, even a soda can.

Up ahead Gabe punctured the raisin box with his pole and called back. "Not very pretty, is it?"

"No."

"Bet you thought you were getting away from this."

The two hours of climbing passed so quickly and easily that before Sarah realized it, they had arrived at 7,700 feet. Sarah had left her watch in Talkeetna and loved the freedom of being without one.

"Okay, everybody, time for a group crevasse check. We'll divide up the area into teams. Poke around your team's area with your ski poles. When you find a bad spot, call out and one of us guides will help you mark it with double wands."

During the crevasse check Sarah asked Tim about the litter.

"You know," he replied, "over nine hundred climbers pass through Kahiltna base camp every year, and apparently some of them don't care what kind of mess they leave behind." Then he raised his voice. "We catch one of you trashing and you'll be shot at dawn." The group applauded.

When the crevasse check was completed, Doug gave the high sign to unrope, and everybody stopped for a snack. Five thousand calories a day was going to take a lot of eating. Sarah knew most people would be thrilled to have to eat that much every day, at least for a couple of weeks, but thanks to her mother's genes, extra pounds had never been one of Sarah's problems.

She was so excited, she had to force herself to eat. She dug through her jacket for the gorp she had stashed earlier. With all the years of family hiking and camping, Sarah had practically been raised on gorp. But it wasn't until she read a mountain-climbing book that she discovered that gorp stood for "good old raisins and peanuts."

As the morning sun warmed up the glacier to sixty degrees, out came the sunglasses and bandannas. Sarah couldn't believe how hot it was. She was actually sweating from just sitting around.

"Hey folks, don't forget the sun lotion and the sunglasses. You'll burn to a crisp, especially on your nose, from that famous glacier glare," Doug said as he lathered sun guard on his face and neck. "Even when it's cloudy, keep your face protected and your eyes covered. Snow blindness has ruined some unlucky climbers' eyes."

Sarah sat down on her pack and stretched out her legs. No worries about Mayurvik or college. Just Sarah against the mountain. Warmed by the sun, she felt her stiff neck and shoulder muscles unwind. She looked around at Camp 1, realizing that Doug was right. This was a much smaller, out-of-the-way spot, compared to the activity down at Kahiltna Glacier.

"Is this terrific or what?" her dad exclaimed as he sat down next to her.

Sarah nodded. She'd never seen him so relaxed. Climbing Mount Hood two summers ago, he'd been in such a rush to get up and down. But on this trip he couldn't set the pace, and he didn't seem to mind. He also seemed to have totally forgotten yesterday's sleeping pad episode and bossing her around about the snowshoes. Sarah had seen him so infrequently since the divorce that she'd forgotten how quick he was to anger, how quick to forget.

"Hey, happy climbers, I hate to break up the party. But if you want to party later, let's get going," Doug yelled out. "We've got to build a cache here and climb back down to base camp. For rookies you are doing a fine job. But let's not push our luck. The midnight sun will be up tonight, but your bodies won't be."

Right before they started climbing, Sarah heard Wendy call out, "Gentlemen, avert your eyes." Sarah looked over and realized that Wendy was going to the bathroom in clear view. But where else could she go? After a respectful amount of time, Sarah went over to Wendy.

"Thank you for saying that."

"What?"

"That gentlemen bit. Before the trip I was advised to announce my intentions and then just do it, but it's so embarrassing."

Wendy smiled and put her arm on Sarah's shoulder. "Hey, I figure that if I get uptight about this, I'll only ruin the trip for myself."

"That's right, Sarah. As they say, there's no gender on the mountain." Sarah blushed in embarrassment at the sound of Doug's voice behind them, but inside she was relieved. At least the ice was broken now and there were two other women on the trip who had to contend with the same thing.

When they started climbing down the mountain, Doug set a slow, steady pace. Sarah felt strong and enjoyed the freedom and ease of climbing. With her empty backpack in the sled, Sarah glided along until the last few minutes when her legs seemed to turn to lead. When they unroped at base camp, she felt oddly relieved to see that even Gabe's face looked tired.

After a leisurely lunch, Sarah decided to rest in the sunshine instead of walking around camp. She wasn't used to being around so many talky people. She noticed that if she closed her eyes, she was pretty much left alone.

Later she and Sam helped Gabe with the chicken *fajita* dinner. But when it was finally ready, they had to wait for Doug's opening remark.

"Folks, we've been eating pretty well here the last couple of days. But from here on out, our menu is based on what we carry. So you might say it's freeze-dried cuisine all the way."

Wendy raised her cup of water. "Here, here. And here's to our first day of climbing." They all raised their cups and cheered. Sarah felt great. She had kept up and hadn't embarrassed herself today. She was part of the group. But then her stomach growled loud enough for those near her to hear.

"Here's to the chow," Sam called out.

Sarah couldn't stop eating. She didn't even look up when Laura sat down beside her. "Hey, Sarah Bear. You're not eating for winter hiberation." Laura's gentle voice relaxed her.

"I don't know. Sounds like a good idea." Then Sarah laughed and took a deep breath. "Thanks. I didn't realize I was eating so fast. I'm just so hungry and tired and . . ."

"Excited? I am. I can't believe I'm finally here. All those years of dreaming and wondering about climbing Denali." Then Laura's voice got somber. "You're lucky to climb it so young."

"Maybe too young . . ." But then Sarah stopped herself. She glanced over and Laura had tears in her eyes. I am lucky, thought Sarah. But why does that upset Laura?

Sarah looked at Laura's long, narrow face with the wrinkles around her green eyes and her long brown hair touched with gray. Probably a little younger than my mother, Sarah thought. But Sarah didn't need another mother. She wanted a friend, a friend for this new adventure. She hadn't had a friend in so long.

"So what's so serious over here? I've had a tremendous day," Wendy said as she joined them, throwing herself down on the pad and still managing to hang on to her bowl. Wendy seemed so comfortable with herself and her body. She reminded Sarah of a Girl Scout counselor with her short, muscular legs, crinkly blue eyes, and a laugh that could be heard all over the glacier.

She laughed like Mike. Maybe that's why her mom had married Mike. There hadn't been much laughter after her dad moved out. And now that Sarah thought about it, not much when he lived with them, either.

"How's it going?" Wendy asked, looking at Sarah.

Sarah knew what she was getting at. "Well, I'm getting better, but it's still hard to change or go to the bathroom knowing that Bobby or some strange guy might walk by at any moment."

"Hey, don't worry," Laura said, resting her hand on Sarah's knee. "It's taking me a while to get used to it too. No matter what Doug says about no gender on the mountain, I'm still a woman, and a bit more modest than Wendy here." Wendy laughed.

"Ah, it'll do you two good to loosen up."

Sarah turned her attention to the rest of the group. Everyone was talking at once. She enjoyed listening, feeling a part of it all. Here she was just another climber, not the all-star girl trying to fit in.

Gabe had already finished eating and was up fooling around with his camera and taking pictures of the glacier, the campsite, and the climbers. When he noticed Sarah watching him, he turned and focused the camera on her. Sarah didn't turn away as she usually did, but instead waved and smiled.

Afterward, Sarah and Tim were on cleanup duty. Scrubbing the pots, he asked, "Well, what did you think of your first day climbing?"

"I loved it. And now that I'm full from dinner, I'm not even tired anymore." Tim looked surprised. "Well, maybe a little." Tim started to laugh, and Sarah jabbed him with a towel. "Okay, okay. So I was a little beat when we first got back here. But hopefully I'm not too tired now to go write in my journal.''

"Great idea. It'll be fun to read over when you're preparing for your next ascent of Denali." Tim laughed again when he saw Sarah's shocked face.

"Didn't you know? You're a lifer now. You'll never get it out of your system." Tim swiped back at her with the dishrag.

"Slow down. I'll settle for just one successful ascent." Sarah grabbed Tim's arm. "How does this compare to other days? Will I be able to keep up? I'm trying not to get worried, but there's so much thinking time during the day. What do you think about?"

"Whoa, so many questions. Of course you'll be able to keep up. You were great today." Tim put away the utensils. "Let's see. I think about how much I love to climb, and I think about my other climbing trips and the people I've known. I think about how lucky I am and that if I'm smart and take precautions. I'll be around for many more climbs. I think about all the great times in my life and all the ones ahead. But mostly I just enjoy myself." Tim turned and looked up at Denali's summit. "Whew, didn't think I could talk so long, did you?"

"Yes, I mean, no." Sarah laughed again. She was always laughing around Tim. She looked at him as he put away the last of the dishes and thought about how he would have great times ahead. He was so positive and determined. Why wasn't he twenty, instead of thirty and about to be married?

"Does Karen climb?"

Just then Bobby walked by. "What are you two KP'ers gabbing about?"

"Climbing. What else?" Tim said as Sarah remained silent, hoping Bobby would get the hint and go away.

40

"Man, one-track minds around here," said Bobby, smiling, as he walked away toward another campsite.

Tim turned back to Sarah. "You asked about Karen. Sure, she climbs. That's how we met. But it's not her whole life like mine. She's an artist, a painter. She's even sold a few paintings in Anchorage."

"Wow. She's lucky." Sarah zipped up her down parka and turned to go. "Tim, it was great today. How can it get better?"

"It does, kid. And it will get worse too. But just wait until the summit." So she was just a kid to Tim. But he kept talking about the summit, as though she really was going to make it.

"You know, Sarah, some people, even ones we thought were very strong, start falling apart right away. You can see it by the very first night." Tim put his arm around Sarah's shoulder. "Look at you. It's been a long day, but you're still hanging in there."

Her dad returned from his walk with Wendy and Laura. "Sarah, I think I'll hit the sack. You ready?"

"Not quite yet. Good night, Dad."

As they finished the cleanup, Sarah felt warm, even though Doug had just announced the temperature had dropped to ten degrees.

The light was still high in the sky, because the midnight sun never set, but suddenly Sarah felt tired. Slowly walking over to the tent, she wondered how sore her legs would feel tomorrow. Tim kept saying they'd grow stronger and stronger each day, so that finally the summit would be just one more climb. He'd better be right, she thought as she fell asleep, too tired after all to write in her journal.

chapter 5

THE next morning, Day 3, Sarah watched the whirlwind breakfast cleanup and packing with amazement. Yesterday's hesitancy had disappeared and a sense of purpose was in the air.

"Folks, our trip up to 7–7 should be easier today because you know the route. We'll carry up the rest of the supplies and the camping equipment and hopefully be there in time for some more major relaxation this afternoon. Of course, that depends on how fast you can set up camp."

As Sarah roped in, Doug came by. "You hung in there well yesterday, Sarah. For a young one I think you might have the instinct of the mountain in you." Sarah couldn't help but smile. Already she had learned that any compliment from Doug, even a backhanded one, was to be treasured. Then Doug turned to the rest of the group. "Folks, let's get cl—imb—ing!"

Bobby let out a holler and called out, "Too bad we

couldn't try it alpine style. We'd be heading up to 10,000 feet right now instead of only up to 7–7.''

Doesn't he ever give up? wondered Sarah. She looked around, and this time Laura winked at her.

Doug didn't wait a beat. "Got an idea, pal. Tomorrow heading up to 10, let's say you carry eighty, a hundred pounds of supplies on your back and the same in your sled. Then you can sit back the next day while we ferry more supplies back and forth. Who'd like to be on Bobby's team tomorrow?" Nobody volunteered, not even Sarah's dad. Sarah looked down at the snow, fearing Bobby would take any glance as approval.

At the team meeting in Talkeetna, Doug had explained they would be switching rope mates around for variety and safety. Today Sarah was roped in with Wendy and Doug.

Once they got started, the fifty-foot span between climbers gave Sarah plenty of solitude to think, except for Doug's frequent pronouncements. His shaggy blond hair peeked out of his hat, and his strong body was fun to watch. But Sarah preferred the silence.

She had always needed time by herself. For an only child, she supposed that was a good thing, but she knew it confused her parents. Ever since she was in third grade or so she'd come home from school and just shut herself up in her room for a while, pulling herself back together. She wasn't extroverted like Gretchen or her dad or Wendy; they all liked being constantly surrounded by people.

Her mother always seemed to understand better, though Sarah knew her silences in Mayurvik worried her. Her mother kept asking Sarah if something was wrong. Of course, something was wrong—she hated her life in Mayurvik. And yet sometimes she had never been happier, like late last summer picking blueberries with her mother high on the tundra above the village or last winter cross-country skiing alone over the hills.

Up in the lead team, Tim followed the wands that Doug had planted the day before. As the sun warmed her body, Sarah's sore limbs began to loosen. But then her feet started to slide on the warmed-over snow, which was just beginning to melt. Sarah remembered Doug's warning in Talkeetna about the snow. "Though June is the best month for climbing Denali because of the weather and prolonged daylight, the snow can be tough to work with."

But Kahiltna Glacier was a mile wide, and even though there were crevasses on either side, Sarah was pretty relaxed going up the middle. She didn't think there was much of a chance she could blow a half-mile margin. But then she remembered that the steerman had done something even more unlikely on the *Exxon Valdez* that March night. Steered right onto Bligh Reef near Valdez when he'd had a three-mile turn area. He'd put a huge hole in the side of the tanker, causing the worst oil spill in history. The pictures of the oil-soaked otters and seals had bothered Sarah the most. Her mother said she'd never seen Sarah so interested in an Alaskan event before and she was right—Sarah never had been.

"Don't get too relaxed, everybody," Doug called out. "Those crevasses are everywhere. One wrong move and that's it."

His shout pulled Sarah out of her thoughts. She'd already seen how oil had muddled the minds of some Alaskans, though if she earned residency she wouldn't refuse the permanent dividend check issued each year to every Alaskan. She knew her check would come from oil money—oil money that she was going to use to help pay for college, wherever that turned out to be.

"Watch your step, Sarah. Didn't you hear what I just

said? You're veering to the right." Sarah looked up to notice her footsteps were off course.

"Not going in a straight line. That's what causes crevasse accidents," Doug continued, shouting at Sarah. Sarah straightened up and moved ahead, wondering if anyone else had heard.

Trying to put her recent mistake out of her mind, she moved along in the beautiful sunshine. With the blue sky and miles of powder snow, she felt as though she were in a ski movie.

After an hour they stopped for a break of crackers, peanut butter, and Tang. It seemed like such an easy day with only an hour more to climb that everyone started fooling around.

Bobby flung a Frisbee Sarah's way, and she returned it right on target, then moved away. She couldn't unwind yet, not until they were safely at Camp 1.

Her dad put on his black Giants baseball hat, and he and Bobby stared pantomiming a game. Her dad sure knew how to relax. He waved her over, and she started cheering as if she were in the cheap seats at Candlestick Park. Soon Sam joined the game as catcher, and Sarah found herself up at bat.

"Folks, I hate to call the game, but I don't like the looks of these clouds," said Doug. "The weather could change on us in fifteen minutes. So let's get moving and hightail it up the mountain and set up camp before we have any more fun. And you'd better put on more layers. It could turn real nasty."

Soon after they started climbing again, Sarah noticed low clouds setting in and light snowflakes flying. Yet it stayed warm. She was sweating in her polar fleece pants. She wanted to rip them off along with her harnesses and sprint up the mountain.

"How can it be so hot and still snow?" Sarah heard

45

Wendy call out. By now, Sarah could see only about a hundred feet in front of her, and she felt as if she were moving through dry ice vapors. The weather change confused her senses and made hearing difficult. Sarah strained to hear Tim's answer and still concentrate on climbing.

"Crazy, isn't it? It's not that cold out and probably beautiful higher up at our camp spot, but these low clouds can really set in down here. Let's just hope we climb out of them."

From back on the third rope team, Sam could be heard singing, "There's a silver lining in every cloud . . ." to the tune of "On a Clear Day."

Laughter rippled up and down the line. But this time Sarah couldn't laugh. She felt disoriented. Not being able to see the snow, she didn't trust her steps.

"Thank God for the wands," Doug yelled out. "They're keeping us on the straight and narrow."

Sarah hated this weather. She wanted to go home, to get out of here. Yesterday and this morning had been so easy compared to this. Now all around her was a gray mist, like the ice fog pictures she'd seen of winter in Fairbanks. Jack had come back from his two weeks with the rural Student Vocational Program in Fairbanks, enjoying his experience working at the *Daily News-Miner,* but not the forty-below weather in January that caused the ice fog, tiny ice crystals formed when the air becomes so cold the moisture freezes. Alaskans put up with the craziest things. She'd take Oregon rain any day.

Sarah remembered the day she'd told Jack she was planning to climb McKinley and how his eyes had sparkled. "On a clear day you can see Denali from the lookout right near the dorm I'll be living in. When I get lonely or frustrated next year, I'll just go look out at the summit and think of you and your journey."

On a clear day. Suddenly they were back at 7–7. It was the same climb as yesterday, but oh, how the weather could make a difference. In the fog she had missed the familiar landmark of Ski Hill, which had let her know they were getting closer to camp yesterday.

They checked the campsite again today for crevasses and then unroped. Sarah hated being tied in, but she appreciated the safety net it offered, thinking again of the woman who had died in the crevasse.

After she took off her pack, Sarah felt as if her body were going to unravel. But she caught herself. They had a camp to put up.

Doug gave out the assignments, spinning around and pointing his finger like a revolving door. "Laura, you and Wendy boil more snow. Tim—you, Sam, and Bobby build the tent platforms. See what you think about snow walls. If this wind continues, we might need them. Gabe, show Sarah and John how to set up our 'throne.'

"But—" Then he slowed down. "Before you get started, bundle up. It looks like the wind is picking up. Get on dry underclothes before you start working. We don't want any hypothermia cases on this expedition." Sarah realized she was shivering, and Doug's suggestion sounded like a very good idea.

Since the tent wasn't up yet, Sarah pulled out a dry shirt from her pack, then stripped off her sweaty layers, grateful she was wearing a sports bra underneath. Because it was bright blue and she'd worn it running, she figured it didn't matter who saw her in it. She put on her clean T-shirt, then her polypro shirt, and finally her polar fleece jacket. Instantly, she felt warmer.

Gabe set Sarah and her dad to work digging a deep

47

hole several hundred feet away from the tents and kitchen area. "After you finish the hole, we'll line it with a garbage sack, to catch the *anaq*." Sarah looked puzzled. "Poop—human, dog, or otherwise." Sarah's dad burst out laughing, and Sarah joined in, despite her embarrassment.

Digging alongside her dad, with only the sound of their shovels crunching against the snow, Sarah enjoyed the closeness. Though her dad didn't say anything, Sarah sensed that he, too, liked the way they were working together. Gabe left to help with the snow walls.

When the hole was complete, her dad suggested building a small snow wall on he side facing the main camp area. Sarah had been camping many times, but never with so little privacy.

"I don't know. There wasn't one at base camp and we're kind of tucked away back here. Why don't we ask Gabe?"

"He's busy."

"Well, then, why don't we just eat lunch and do it later, if necessary?"

"No, I want to do the job right the first time around." Sarah wondered whether to help out or walk away and feed her starving body.

"Hey, John, don't bother with that. Just a waste of energy," Doug said, as he walked over.

"Why not?" Sarah's dad kept digging.

Doug smiled his all-purpose smile. "Hey, we're all family. You'll soon find that living together twenty-four hours a day and depending on each other for every little thing, any need for privacy just disappears."

Sarah stood up and waited to see if her dad would stop. Finally, he stood up. "Let's go. I'm hungry and we've still got our tent to set up," was all he said.

Sarah went over to get some more gorp and returned to find her dad already had the tent halfway up.

At lunch Doug had to bang on a pot several times to get the group's attention. "Not bad, guys. Two and a half hours for your second camp setup. In another few days, I predict you seasoned climbers will pull it off in under two hours."

After lunch the weather was too poor to stay out, so Sarah thought about writing in her journal. But she was so frustrated and muddled by the change in weather she didn't know what to say.

So, instead, she lay on her sleeping bag and stretched out her legs, trying to relax. After a while she pulled out *Wuthering Heights*, and soon she was engrossed in the turmoils of Catherine and Heathcliff high on the English moors, far away from the snows of Denali.

In the late afternoon, the weather cleared up slightly, but not enough to get Sarah outdoors. When Sam came back to the tent, Sarah closed her novel and looked up. "Sam, it's good to see you. You'll cheer me up," she said, sitting up and smiling. "Tell me how you ended up on this mountain. Everybody knows all about Dad and me."

Sarah rolled over and stretched out on her stomach, her chin in her hands, and listened, watching Sam gesture with his big hands as he talked. "Two years ago I got tired of being fat and full of nicotine. So I lost thirty pounds and stopped smoking. I figured if I could do that, I could do anything, even climb McKinley. So here I am. I've still got some pounds to go, but I feel great."

Sarah sat up. "Aren't you worried about altitude sickness?"

"Nope. I am not going to worry about anything until

I have to. I'll just take one day at a time. Why? Are you?"

"Yes. Altitude sickness is the number one reason climbers don't make the summit. And I'll die if I don't make the summit. But I've always gotten motion sickness since I was a kid. Car, train, boat—anything that moves makes me sick to my stomach. What if altitude sickness is like that?"

"Motion sickness is all in the head. I've told you that before, Sarah." Sarah hadn't heard her dad outside the tent. Unzipping the door, he bowed his head and stepped in. "And I'll bet altitude sickness is the same thing. Climbers get scared. It's as simple as that."

Before Sarah could respond, Sam spoke. "Oh, I don't know about that, John. Some of the stories I've read about McKinley climbs sound pretty rough. Altitude sickness can strike anyone. Nausea, headaches, too weak to walk. It's more than just a head trip." Sam paused for a moment and then said, "Well, I think I'll get some fresh air."

Only later did Sarah realize that her dad hadn't answered Sam back. Sam hadn't given him the chance—he knew when to make an exit. I should learn something from this, she thought, as she looked across at her dad eating dinner.

chapter 6

SARAH tossed and turned all night, bothered by the wind hitting the walls of the tent. Now,
lying awake in the early morning light, she figured they
would be in for their first bad weather day. What would
she do all day inside this domed tent, five by eight and
only four feet high?

After last night's eight o'clock radio report from base
camp forecasted poor weather at 7–7, Doug told them
they didn't have to rush out of the sack, unless Tim or
Gabe gave the high sign or the sun was burning a hole
in the tent. Sarah sat up and sighed. Neither of those
things appeared to be happening.

Both Sam and her dad were still snoring, so Sarah
dug out *Wuthering Heights* again. When her dad and
Sam didn't awake, in spite of the wind, Sarah figured
it must be earlier than she thought. Since she couldn't
possibly sleep, it was back to the tangled lives of all
the Earnshaws and Lintons.

About an hour later Tim called into their tent, and finally Sam and her dad woke up. "Doesn't look good. The winds are blowing hard, and it's impossible to see even a few feet. Looks like it will be a good day to rest up. Come out for breakfast when you feel like it and we'll discuss the options.

What options? thought Sarah. A day spent cooped up in this tent with Emily Brontë? Sarah wanted to get moving, away from all this. Her dad sat up, rubbed his eyes, and said, "Good morning."

"I don't know what's good about it." She looked over at her dad. "How could you and Sam sleep with the whipping tent flaps?"

"Honey, they warned us this could happen."

Sarah shook her head. "Not this early. Up near the summit, maybe. But I'm prepared to climb, not sit around. If you knew so much about this, you should have warned me."

"And you're the one who said you'd never get frustrated with me again, if I'd let you come." Sarah glared at her dad. He was always bringing up the past.

Sam crawled over to the door, and suddenly Sarah realized he'd heard the whole discussion. Furious, she waited until her dad left, and then she pulled out her baby wipes.

Maybe freshening up a bit would improve her mood. She washed her face and hands, then under her arms. It couldn't replace a shower, but it would have to do. She tried to comb through her long, tangled hair, afterward pulling it back and braiding it in one long braid. Already it felt dirty. Outside, she heard Doug's voice.

"In this kind of wind the next safe campsite is at 10,000 feet. That's a long three-and-a-quarter-mile climb with an elevation gain of 2,300 feet and a lot tougher than what we've already experienced."

Sarah tried to dress quickly, listening carefully as she zipped up her coat. The thermometer on her coat read five degrees, but she knew the windchill factor made it much colder. Sarah would have loved to stay inside the tent, but her stomach was growling.

"That's a six to eight hour climb, and if we can't make it, we'll find ourselves camping on some windy, dangerous slope, plus the visibility is simply not good enough right now. So"—Doug looked around, trying to coax smiles out of the group—"let's just relax today. Play a few cards, sleep a little, and rest up for the assault ahead." Only Wendy smiled at his use of "assault" instead of "ascent." Even Gabe's tanned face was scrunched into a frown, Sarah noticed.

Doug went around pounding people on the back. "Hey, guys, this is nothing. I'll bet up above 12 the sun is blazing. These low-flying suckers are formed by the sun evaporating water off the lower glaciers, rivers, and lakes. They'll be gone by evening."

Sarah didn't care where these clouds came from, she just wanted them to go away—now. She said little at breakfast and then quickly walked back to the tent, avoiding everyone and anxious to get warm. She'd known it was going to be a physical struggle. But the waiting, the psychological part, she wasn't yet ready for.

Pulling off her top two layers, she nestled down into her sleeping bag and pulled out her journal. She'd put it off long enough. But somehow she didn't know how to get started. Without thinking, she told herself to just open to the first page and start listing all the things she could be doing right now that would be worse than waiting it out in a tent on Denali.

- taking the SATs
- fighting with my mother
- being a POW in solitary confinement
- starving to death
- being paralyzed, homeless, deaf

This was too depressing, she thought. Why did I come on this expedition?

Writing again, she listed:

- test my physical strength
- get out of Mayurvik
- prove something to my dad

Sarah shut the journal. This wasn't working. It was her mother, the English teacher, who loved journals, thought Sarah. She liked doing math problems because there was always an answer, a right answer, or proving a hypothesis in a science experiment. Journals were for feelings, and feelings got too messy. Except the year before in Eugene, when she had loved writing in her journal in Ms. Harris's creative writing class, her favorite time of the day.

Sarah opened the journal again and, for the first time, noticed the inscription in the front. Crying, her hand shaking, her mother had handed Sarah this journal right before Sarah got on the plane in Mayurvik to fly into Anchorage to meet her dad for the expedition. ''Read the quote in the front,'' her mother had said. ''It's from Wendell Berry, one of my favorite nature writers. It will make you brave." Sarah had hugged her mother and then she had started crying too.

> *"Always in the big woods when you leave familiar ground and step off alone into a new place there will be, along with the feelings of curiosity and excitement, a little nagging dread. It is the ancient fear of the unknown and it is your first bond with the wilderness you are going into."*

Oh, there was fear all right, especially today. Funny her mom should pick this quote. Her mom who always seemed so together, but private and conservative, never much of a risk-taker. Not like Ms. Harris, who was so free and open about her search for self-knowledge.

Ms. Harris didn't act as though she had all the answers. She'd studied Jungian psychology and mythology and all sorts of things. She'd bring these ideas into class and have the students write, prompting their unconscious thoughts from deep within themselves.

Sarah used to laugh to herself when she thought how the parents and administrators would die if they knew what Ms. Harris's students were doing. They weren't writing obscene sexual thoughts—at least, she wasn't—but, rather, beautiful, personal prose and poetry that had never had a place in any of Sarah's classes before. She was exploring her inner self and she felt lucky, so lucky, that Ms. Harris would risk teaching them this way.

Sarah had no interest at all in creative writing, but her schedule wasn't working out and she needed an English elective. Gretchen tried to talk her into taking drama, but Sarah knew she definitely didn't belong on the stage. So she promised the counselor she'd try creative writing for one day. That first day in class, Ms. Harris started talking about the Greek and Roman gods and goddesses, and the feminine and masculine poles and how they were reflected in people and in literature.

Sarah immediately felt that she was Artemis, the huntress who fought for equality and friendship, her body chiseled into a toughened fighter ready for any battle. Artemis didn't need men for romance; instead, she wanted male and female companionship to help fulfill her dreams.

Just last month, Sarah had written to Ms. Harris to tell her about her McKinley trip. Ms. Harris had written right back, encouraging Sarah just as she had encouraged her a year ago when Sarah had come to her in tears. Sarah could still see Ms. Harris standing in the classroom with her long, dark hair pulled back with a beaded barrette, wearing a long denim skirt and embroidered vest with tights and Berkenstock sandals.

"Sarah, I know how awful you must feel. Let yourself be sad for a while. But a think about how much you will learn in Alaska—about living in a native culture, about winter life in the outdoors, about finding strength within yourself when loneliness comes."

Sarah hadn't wanted to think about what she would learn. She wanted to stay at South Eugene High School.

Sarah pulled out Ms. Harris's letter from the back of the journal.

Sarah, just remember that all of us must take a mythical journey if we want to discover who we really are. You are so very lucky to have a physical challenge to lead you on that journey. You will confront many obstacles on the mountain and have to integrate your shadow self to complete your journey. But like all the goddesses, I know you

*will do it. I envy you to be getting this opportunity
at such a young age. How strong you will be when
you return.*

Ms. Harris had always believed in her from the very
first day and made her feel special. So why this morning, facing her first obstacle, couldn't she feel as excited
about her journey as Ms. Harris?

Sarah put down the journal and started rummaging
through the food bag, pulling out a candy bar. Just then
Wendy showed up outside the tent. "Hi, can I come
in?"

"Sure," Sarah said, unwrapping the bar and taking
a bite. "It must be freezing out there."

Wendy nodded and shivered. "Frustrated?" Sarah
nodded, her mouth full. "Me, too. If I sit in that tent all
day, I'll just eat. The original stress eater, that's me."

But I'm not a stress eater like you, Sarah wanted to
say. I never gain weight. I don't wear my emotions all
over my sleeve. Sarah wished Wendy hadn't come by.

"Come on over to our tent and play hearts with
Laura and me."

"I don't know how to play hearts."

"Sarah, I've offered to teach you many times. But
you always get frustrated." There was her dad again,
piping up from outside the tent.

Sarah wanted to say, I get frustrated because you
constantly criticize my plays. Instead, she took another
bite of the candy bar and glared at him just as he, Sam,
and Bobby crowded into the tent.

"I'm in," said Sam, moving into a comfortable position on his sleeping bag.

"Me, too. hearts is my game." Everything was Bobby's game.

Wendy looked at Sarah and shrugged her shoulders,

but didn't look fazed at all. "Count me in, too." Why should Wendy be fazed? She probably had a dad who thought everything she did was terrific.

"But I thought you said Laura wanted to play. Shouldn't somebody go get her?" Sarah said, looking around.

"Nah. I'm sure she'll enjoy some quiet time to read. I just told her I was going out to find some action."

"It's pretty scrunched in here," Sarah said, moving toward the door. "I'll go see what the guides are up to."

"There's plenty of room," Bobby said, moving over and patting the spot next to him. "Here's a place marked especially with your name."

Sarah knew that if she stomped off now she'd look like a baby. But if she played, she'd look like a fool. "Well, just for a little while."

Wendy whispered some pointers on how to pass cards, and Sarah played it safe. So by the middle of the game, when Tim stopped by, she had also kept her cool.

"Hey, glad to see you're having fun. But don't forget to drink, even on a day like this when you're not doing much. Add the Nutrasweet, if that's the only way you can take it. That's better than the sugar drinks, which cause the 'flash and crash' cycle, as Doug calls it. We can't afford to have any moody climbers." Sarah felt that he was looking straight at her, but then he smiled.

"Tim, why don't you join us?" Sarah figured that with Tim around, Bobby and her dad would stay on their best behavior.

"Nah, looks like you've got a full house."

"Then take my place. I hardly have any points."

"No, thanks. But I will borrow a book. Believe it or not, I forgot to bring one."

"Well, I'm already into the wilds of *Wuthering*

Heights, but you can borrow my copy of *Catcher in the Rye.* My mom wanted to send along the whole college classics reading list.''

''Hey, Sarah, you're a Holden Caulfield fan? He's one of my favorite characters.''

Sarah started laughing and so did everybody else. Everybody but Bobby.

They played hearts for four hours, stopping only for latrine runs and a short break for lunch inside the tent. Sarah ended up having a good time and was actually proud of herself. She didn't lose her temper, not even when Bobby gloated over winning. Every time her dad started to say something about her playing, Wendy put her hand on Sarah's leg, or Sam made a joke.

Bobby wanted to start up a new game and the others agreed, except Sarah. ''No thanks, it looks like its warmed up a bit, so I'm taking a walk.''

''Where to?'' her dad asked.

''Round and round the tents, I guess, and then I'll visit Laura.''

Wendy offered to join her, but Sarah shook her head. ''Oh, no, you play some more with the guys. They need your calming influence.'' What Sarah really needed was to be alone, alone, alone. This was only Day 4.

chapter 7

"UP and at 'em, folks. I know it's the middle of the night. But the weather report says it's going to be hot today, so let's beat the heat." Sarah jerked awake and rolled over. Her dad was gone. Still wrapped in her sleeping bag, she quickly unzipped the tent door and looked around. No activity. Where was Doug's voice coming from? Then she swiveled her head over to the kitchen area. Everybody was up and talking loudly. What time *was* it? Could it be Day 5 already? Right now, Sarah wished she hadn't given up her watch in Talkeetna.

It seemed like just moments ago she couldn't sleep, tossing and turning, trying not to wake her dad. She had lain looking up at the dome ceiling, unable to close her eyes. Her body had shut down but not off. Now everybody was up, but her.

Sarah sat up and tried to dress, but her hands were shaking so hard she could barely pull on her clothes.

Yet already she could feel her body unwinding, her shoulders loosening, her legs begging to climb. She should feel tired, but instead she was thrilled they would be climbing again. Sarah's stomach started making noises. She was starving, yet she knew it wasn't actually breakfast time. All that snacking yesterday must have stretched her stomach.

Finally reaching the kitchen area, she hurriedly poured some instant oatmeal into her Sierra cup and started stirring it. "Good morning, sleepyhead," her dad said from behind. "You ready for Day 5?"

"Is it morning yet? What time is it?" Sarah said, rubbing her eyes. "Why didn't you wake me up?" Just then Doug took his vaulted position on top of a camp stool.

"I thought you needed your beauty sleep." Her dad smiled, then moved away, closer to Doug.

"Hey, happy campers, yesterday you survived your first bad weather day." The group applauded and Bobby and Wendy whistled. "And now I'm dragging you out at three A.M. to start climbing. I should have warned you, but with yesterday's weather, there was no way to tell what today would bring. But it's clear, and later it's supposed to get so hot we'd sweat to death, plus never make it in the soft, mushy snow. So today is your lucky day. Not only do we get to climb in the middle of the night, but we get to break camp again." More cheering and applauding.

Everybody was so anxious to get started that Sarah hardly had time for any more breakfast. Since it was so early, though, she knew she would have plenty of hours later to eat. Bobby came trekking by with a big smile, the smile that curled up his thin upper lip but left the surly bottom one to flounder. "Didn't want to leave you behind, princess."

Sarah could have punched him, but instead she smiled sweetly, and rushed over to the tent to stuff her sleeping bag and pack up her things. Her dad was talking to Doug, so Sarah began helping Sam dismantle the tent. Sarah liked the way they worked in silent synchronization, Sam whistling in the background. If she were working with her dad, he would be giving her step-by-step instructions, even though she'd taken down the tent many times before by herself.

Looking up after she and Sam finished, Sarah noticed that her dad and Bobby were taking down the other tent, while Wendy and Laura helped pack up the kitchen. They seemed to be getting in each other's way. Yet her dad didn't say much, letting Bobby do the talking. Why can't he ever act that way with me? she wondered.

When he was finished, Sarah followed her dad over to tie up the big garage sack lining the latrine hole. Then they took shovels and covered up the hole with mounds of snow. She expected her dad to make some joke the way Bobby would have done, but instead they worked in silence, getting the messy job over with as quickly as possible. Gabe brought over their harnesses, and they roped together and walked to the lip of a deep crevasse, throwing the black garbage bag down into it. "There she goes," her dad said softly.

Before this year, Sarah knew she would have been disgusted by this duty. But using "honey buckets" in Mayurvik this past winter when the plumbing pipes froze had trained her well and made her more appreciative of modern conveniences. In March, while playing in the basketball tournament in Anchorage, Sarah had almost felt guilty using water out of the tap and flushing the toilet.

When the job was complete and they had walked

back to safer ground, her father looked around and let out a long whistle. "Isn't this something?"

Startled, Sarah followed his gaze. In her frazzled state this morning she'd completely forgotten the scenery. Though they could no longer see Denali's summit, hundreds of little gray and blue mountains surrounded the white, sweeping glacier.

Ah, thought Sarah, forgetting this morning's frustrations. How few people would ever see this incredible view.

Before the rest of the group put on their harnesses, Doug gave final instructions. With a big sweep of his right hand, he pointed up the mountain. "The big challenge today is the tough thousand-foot climb up Ski Hill. Then we climb on up to the base of Kahiltna Pass to 10,000 feet, or even on to 11,000 feet depending on the weather. There we'll set up Camp 2 and go back to sleep." Sarah prayed her legs were ready.

She loved the feel of the ski poles in her hands again. In just a couple of days, climbing had almost become a part of her, and she had missed it yesterday. Conquering the mountain was so exhilarating. Sarah was roped in the front team today, in the middle spot between Doug and Bobby. She liked the feeling of power that climbing on the lead team gave her.

She'd felt powerless for so long, ever since her parents' divorce four years ago. Sarah now realized that up until the divorce she'd been the one in control; her parents' whole life had revolved around her needs. Was she eating right? Did she need a ride? Was the track coach giving her enough attention?

The beginning climb was steep, but not slippery. At four A.M. the sun was out, though it was still cold, about zero degrees. Sarah breathed hard, planting her poles carefully at every step. Her sled was sliding easily, but her legs were tired, her hips sore. Tim was right. Even one day without exercise could set you back a bit.

As she moved along, Sarah thought about how her dad must be enjoying this power too. With both her and her mother gone, he had no one to boss around at home. Now that he was on the road and no longer supervising the sales crew, he had no one to boss at work, either.

"Don't forget we're heading toward the eastern part of the glacier to avoid those crevasses hidden right up the center," Doug called out. "It's a longer route, but worth the trouble." When Bobby didn't respond, Doug turned around, but Bobby only looked down. Sarah breathed a sigh of relief. Maybe today Bobby would be quiet for once.

Ski Hill gradually lost its steepness, and Sarah began to feel stronger, moving effortlessly. Kahiltna Pass slowly came into view, even though it would be two to three more hours before they reached it. At the refreshment break, Sarah fed off the group's enthusiasm as Sam and Wendy planned a mini-celebration for lunch in honor of the group's surviving their first bad weather day.

Sarah marveled at how those two never slowed down, or when they did, how they bounced back so quickly. But sometimes they came on too strong, and it was then that she appreciated the quiet contentment of Gabe, sitting alone looking at the mountain, or Laura's calmness as she talked quietly with Tim.

By mid-morning the sun had warmed to sixty degrees, so at the next break Sarah took off her polar fleece pants and top and climbed just in her polypro outfit. Doug was right. By mid-afternoon it would be sweltering out here, like a Florida hothouse, as Wendy called it. Sarah hated this constant changing in and out of clothes, but with no prospect of a shower for days sweating was worse.

An hour later, when Kahiltna Pass loomed closer, Doug stopped the group and insisted they change back into their heavier clothes. "The winds can be brutal up here. Dress for them and get ready to build strong snow walls." Sure enough, thirty minutes later the wind was blowing twenty miles an hour, and Sarah's wind suit never felt better.

As the morning dragged on, however, Kahiltna Pass seemed no closer. Where was the ease from earlier today, the flow she had felt? One step, one step, Sarah kept repeating, to push forward legs that just didn't want to move.

Suddenly Tim's words from last winter flooded into her mind. "Climbing can be drudgery at times. You have to be ready for that too. When I first started climbing as a teenager, the monotony drove me crazy—until I reached my first summit and felt the incredible exhilaration."

Sarah fell into a routine, focusing her mind so that her body felt as if it were floating above her. She moved forward, concentrating on the snow, trying not to think about her tired legs, a warm bath, or a hot plate of enchiladas.

Even Sarah's dad looked exhausted when they finally arrived at Camp 2 at 10,000 feet. The group decided to snack first, then set up the camp with a late lunch after that. Better to get the hard labor over with, Sarah agreed. After lunch, Wendy and Sam got everyone telling ghost stories, which they topped off with haunted instant chocolate pudding for dessert. Sarah's body didn't know if it was day or night. She could hardly keep her eyes open, so she went back to the tent.

Sarah fell asleep wishing every day could be like

today. She had hit a groove. She had gotten through the rough climb by focusing herself and relaxing, and even enjoying the scenery before she became exhausted.

She lay in her sleeping bag thinking that since the trip had begun, this morning was the first time she'd felt a high, something like the effortless workout she used to experience while running. She'd hoped to feel the climber's high on this trip, but with all the drudgery and hard work she wasn't sure it would happen.

Some time later Sarah woke up shaking. Yet she wasn't cold. She'd been dreaming about running around Hayward Field in the state meet, coming around the last curve in the mile race in third place. She was smiling. She was gaining on the other two runners. Suddenly her leg cramped. She slowed down. One girl passed her, then another and another, until finally she was in eighth place, way back from the leaders as she crossed the finish line. In tears she looked up to the stands, where her mother was waving and cheering and her dad sat with a frown on his face.

A far cry from when Sarah was younger and beating girls much older than she in the fun races. That's all her dad would let her enter, swearing he didn't want her burnt out by the time she was out of high school. But then she found out how addicting winning could be. When you were twelve and the fastest middle-school runner in Eugene, it was hard not to love the attention. Running was king in Eugene, the track capital of America.

It wasn't the first time she'd been beaten. Yet before last year she'd been so used to winning, the new Mary Decker Slaney they had called her. She used to see Mary grocery shopping in Eugene with her daughter, and think, I can still be a world-class runner when I'm thirty, just like she is, and have a family too. However, when other girls started beating her on a regular basis, she became desperate. Okay, so she wasn't fast anymore. Then she'd be strong and steady, a long-distance pro in the marathon. Like Joan Benoit Samuelson she'd win the Olympic marathon someday.

Then the disastrous marathon in San Francisco, up and down scenic hills until she hit the wall at twenty-two miles and had to drop out. Everybody thought she had been crazy to try—her high school coach, her dad, Gretchen. And her mom would have, too, if anyone had told her. Her failed marathon . . . it was probably the number-one reason Sarah was climbing Denali right now. But this time she would show everyone she could go the distance.

chapter 8

DAY 6 dawned clear, but not very sunny. After quickly eating breakfast and dismantling the tents because of the wind, Doug got them off to an early start around six o'clock. Sarah was thankful that it was not the middle of the night. It would be a tough day— back down to 7–7 for supplies, then the long, steep climb again to 10—but she felt rested and ready to go and knew more what to expect. Yet she wondered— what did the weather have in store today?

Sarah loved hiking down the mountain with no weight to pull in the sled. It almost made the double-back trips worth it. Doug, Tim, and Gabe carried a little bit of food and some emergency supplies, but Sarah traveled burden-free. Because of that and the downhill course, she didn't have to work so hard. Everyone else seemed more relaxed on these return trips, too, except maybe Bobby and her dad, who always wanted to push on.

They ate an early lunch at Camp 1, then loaded up the rest of the supplies. With her pack and heavy sled, Sarah felt as though they were making little progress as they climbed back up. Her pack got heavier and heavier.

Her stomach began aching, and all she could think of was food and a warm bed, especially when the wind picked up. Food—that was what she wanted. Chinese food. Chicken chow mein, ginger beef, bean sprouts, crisp bean pods, sweet and sour pork, wonton soup, fortune cookies, and afterward a huge chocolate milk shake.

A slog. That's what Tim called it and he was right. Slogging along, Sarah started feeling sorry for herself. There were so many other, better things she could be doing right now. Finally, out of nowhere appeared Camp 2 at 10,000 feet. "The wind can be a killer up here," Doug warned as they pulled in. "Tonight you'd better reinforce your walls. Make 'em strong—and I mean *strong*."

Just when Sarah thought she could relax, they had to do more. If only they hadn't had to take the tents down this morning because of the wind. To top it off, her dad announced that since it was late he and Doug were going to prepare dinner, while the rest of them set up the tents. "Bobby's going to be in our tent tonight, so you two can set it up."

"I can't believe this," Sarah said, wiping her face with her yellow bandanna. "You don't want to be stuck working with me, and Bobby's been getting on everybody's nerves, so you throw the rotten apples together. Thanks a lot."

Sarah shrugged off her father's conciliatory arm hug, as Bobby walked up.

"Okay, darlin', ready to go?"

"I'm not darling, even to my dad, and I didn't know you were from the South."

"Well, excuse me," said Bobby, walking away.

While they worked, the winds grew stronger. Even with her down parka on, Sarah was shaking, her fingers too numb to fiddle with the poles. So when Bobby worked quickly and efficiently, it was hard to stay mad at him.

"I think we'd better reinforce these snow walls some more, Bobby," Sarah said, as he pounded the last tent picket into the snow.

"Nah, this is good enough. They're the same as the others. Worked fine last night."

"But the winds are blowing much harder tonight." Sarah almost had to shout for Bobby to hear her.

Bobby motioned with his arm. "Come on, let's go eat. I'm starving and you look on the verge of hypothermia. We can check it out later."

Sarah stood there examining the walls, wondering what to do when she heard her dad call dinner. Hot food would warm her up.

Huddled with the others for warmth and company, Sarah concentrated on eating her freeze-dried chili. It wasn't the Chinese food she'd dreamed of, but it would do.

"Hello, Sarah." Somehow Gabe had the ability to make her feel alone with him even in these close quarters. Is that how Yup'ik families survived in their small homes, by making their own private space?

"Hi. I sure am hungry."

Gabe raised his eyebrows, then took another bite. At least I understand that, thought Sarah. Raised eyebrows meant yes in the Yup'ik culture, something she'd figured out quite early on when she realized that all the communication in the village wasn't verbal.

After a few moments of eating, Gabe spoke in a serious voice. "Sarah, I've noticed your snow walls aren't very high. Would you like me to help you build them up more after dinner?"

"It's funny you mention them. I was just telling Bobby—"

"Hey, what's going on over there?" Doug's angry voice carried over the wind. He was pointing to where a snow wall had collapsed into the side of Sarah's tent.

"That's our tent!" her father yelled, running over.

Sarah turned angrily toward Bobby. She should have followed her gut instinct to reinforce the walls instead of giving in to Bobby's laziness.

Sarah didn't even try to explain to her dad what had happened. But then, when he didn't flare up at her, she hoped he knew the truth. Sarah was furious inside. She wanted to blame Bobby, yet she had to admit that she had been cold and hungry, too, and somewhat relieved to take advantage of Bobby's earlier excuse.

After helping Bobby and her dad rebuild the walls and secure the tent, Sarah went looking for Laura, Wendy, and Sam. They would cheer her up. Instead, Gabe was the only one in the kitchen area. She still felt shy around him.

"Tent and walls all fixed up?" he asked, finishing the dishes.

Sarah nodded. "Thanks for the offer, but unfortunately it came too late."

"Everybody makes mistakes and shows weakness sometimes."

"Not you. You always seem in control. Calm and careful, so sure about what to do."

"That's how I am? Good." Gabe laughed—a joyful, sincere laugh. It reminded Sarah of Jack's laugh. "Maybe they'll let me come again."

"Of course they will."

"You know, I'm only an apprentice guide on this trip. I've never climbed Denali before."

"But all your climbing experience proves your ability."

"I did climb a lot in college, all over the Chugach Mountains and other places around Anchorage."

"Gabe, why aren't there more Alaska Native climbers?"

"Why aren't there more women climbers?"

Sarah smiled and nodded. "You're right. It does seem to be mostly guys, white and middle-aged at that."

"With time and money." Gabe paused for a moment and Sarah was afraid he would stop talking. She loved listening to the rhythmic pattern of his speech. "I am Yup'ik Eskimo. I love to climb. But part of me also wishes I were home salmon fishing right now. Do you know what the month of June means in Yup'ik?" Sarah shook her head. "*Kaugun,* the hitting of fish." Gabe started walking and Sarah joined him.

"I don't think most Yup'iks would climb a mountain just to get to the top. If I were to climb this mountain to go hunting, that would make sense to the elders. But just to do it, no. We don't believe in challenging nature; we believe in abiding by her rules and respecting her dangers as well as admiring her beauty."

Sarah nodded her head. She had noticed how the villagers hadn't seemed to curse nature when bad weather came, but instead made the best of it.

"Some people like to climb for the thrill, the competition. I don't look at competition the same way."

"Then why did you come?" Gabe and Sarah stood close together, trying to shelter themselves from the wind.

Gabe shrugged his shoulders and Sarah waited for what seemed like minutes, praying he would keep talking. It had taken Sarah a while in Mayurvik before she learned how to wait for a response, and not just jump in at the first little lull in the conversation.

"In college, living in Anchorage amidst the concrete and buildings, I could get away when I climbed, and pretend I was hunting on the tundra." Gabe pulled up the fur ruff on his down parka. "I need to be outdoors. Working for my region's corporation offices in Anchorage is confining at times. I get frustrated and lonely for my village."

"Where are you from, Gabe?"

"Peñarmiut. Not too far from Mayurvik, except that we're on the coast, actually up on the cliffs overlooking the Bering Sea. Peñarmiut—people of the cliffs."

"What a beautiful name. What does Mayurvik mean in Yup'ik?"

"Let's see." Gabe paused, thinking, then answered, "Mayurvik. A place to go up to in the hills or the mountains, to live or maybe just to camp. I think they worried about the river flooding over there, so they built the village up high."

"Mayurvik. That seems right. I used to love looking down from the hills onto the Kuskokwim River. And now here we are camping in the mountains."

"*Ii-i*," Gabe said and nodded. He kept walking around the tents. With the wind blowing, Sarah had to strain to hear his words. She didn't want this to end. "I always climbed the highest cliffs during hunting season. So what other way was there to get out in Anchorage, but join the mountaineering club at the university?"

"How exciting." Sarah thought maybe she would join one in college.

73

"No, really more like survival, until I got hooked on it. So now I am missing fish camp. My parents and all my brothers and sisters will be there with their kids."

"Maybe you can visit after our expedition and the salmon will still be running?"

Gabe shook his head. "If all goes well on this one, they have me booked for trips all summer."

"But what about your job?"

"The corporation gave me the summer off."

"That's great." But Sarah couldn't tell if Gabe was happy about it or not.

"So you live in Mayurvik?" Suddenly Sarah realized the wind had stopped. The others in the tents would be able to hear them talking.

"This year." Sarah blushed in embarrassment. Had she said anything that offended him?

"I heard you talking about it to Wendy and Laura."

"I thought they might understand, since they're teachers in Anchorage."

"But Anchorage is not Mayurvik."

Sarah nodded. "I was confused living there. I didn't fit in."

Sarah's dad poked his head out of the tent. "Hello, Gabe." Gabe gave a slight nod.

"Sarah, pretty cold out there. Don't you think it's time to hit the sack? It's been a tough couple of days."

"All right. Good night, Gabe." Sarah wanted to shake Gabe's hand, like the villagers did when they first met someone or saw someone after a long absence, but she hesitated because her dad was watching. As Gabe turned to go, she stopped him. "Gabe, how do you say good night in Yup'ik?"

"*Piuraa.*"

"*Piuraa,* Gabe," Sarah said, knowing she didn't

74

have the correct guttural sound, but Gabe smiled anyway.

"*Piuraa,* Sarah."

When Sarah entered the tent, her dad asked, "What were you talking about?" Her dad always wanted to know everything about Sarah's life, even though he never shared anything from his own.

"We were talking about Mayurvik." Sarah looked around the tent. "Where's' Bobby?"

"Oh, he's off socializing. You know, Sarah, I wouldn't tell him too much. You've been so negative about your life there, and he might take it personally."

"Thank you, Dad, for that advice from Ann Landers. I'll keep it in mind."

Soon, as if their last exchange hadn't bothered him a bit, Sarah's dad was snoring loudly.

Sarah changed into a clean T-shirt, wondering if she was too negative. Just because her dad was, did she have to imitate his worst trait?

Sarah lay in her sleeping bag, listening to the wind start up again. With her right arm extended up, she curled her fingers into a rabbit like she'd done as a kid. In spite of the midnight sun, she could make out a faint rabbit shadow against the ceiling of the tent. Shadow— the shadow self Ms. Harris had talked about. You had to integrate and accept your shadow as part of your being or you would never be whole.

The shadow, the little bag you pull behind, full of all the negative stuff society or you, yourself, say isn't good about you. Her shadow, getting bigger and bigger every year. It had tripled in size in Mayurvik. She didn't want to pull her shadow behind her all the way up Denali. But how was she supposed to make it part of herself?

75

SARAH woke out of a dead sleep, freezing, her toes so numb she couldn't feel them. She tried wriggling them around in the vapor barrier inside her sleeping bag to warm them up, but that didn't seem to help. Not only was she colder than she'd ever been but there was a different feel in the air, as if the cold were creeping into every opening in the tent.

Tim had warned her last winter to expect to be cold at times and to prepare for it. But she hadn't known how to prepare. What was she supposed to do? Go out and freeze on the tundra? She had asked her mother for suggestions.

"Sarah, it sounds like practicing for labor to me. When I was pregnant with you, your dad tried to prepare me for the pain of labor by pinching me. But I always yelled, 'Stop.' It's pretty hard to put up with pain when you don't have to."

"So, what happened? Was it bad?"

"Of course. But like all mothers say, you forget it the minute the baby comes into the world. You were such a beautiful baby."

Day 7, already a week into the trip. That should make me feel better, thought Sarah as she quickly pulled on her clothes. She and her dad left the tent together, hurrying over to the kitchen area to pour some hot Tang into their cold bodies. No more coffee, Doug had said last night. "Caffeine does strange things to people at this altitude. And we're strange enough as it is . . ." Sarah had laughed, but it *was* strange up here, like being on another planet, bugs from another world. What was happening in the real world?

After drinking the hot liquid, Sarah felt better, although she was still not warm. The thermometer read five below, but with the windchill it felt like twenty-five below. No wonder she was so cold. As she packed up her sled in the blowing wind, Sarah felt as though she were working in freeze-dried motion.

"Let's get out of here quickly," Doug called out. "Climbing's got to be better than this."

For the first hour Sarah moved in silence, her arms and legs stiff as if frozen cuts of beef. Tim kept turning around to check on her. Slowly her limbs began to thaw out. Trying to get her mind off her body, Sarah concentrated on identifying crevasses. From far away they looked like small holes, but up close they were miles across. She remembered the first day and how they looked from the air. She shivered at the thought of her body rolling silently into a crevasse, swallowed by the frozen, silent North, without anyone ever knowing what happened to her.

After three hours they reached Camp 3 at 11,000 feet, a small area with only a narrow band of flat land smooth enough for tents and supposedly protected from the wind. They took a short snack break of cheese and crackers, and then unloaded their sleds and set aside the supplies. No one was in the mood to hang around, so they left right away.

The descent went quickly enough except that Sarah still couldn't get warm. No matter how hard she pushed, she couldn't sweat, and the wind blew through her as if she were full of cracks. That's it, she thought. I'm cracking up.

When they finally arrived back at 10 two hours later, Sarah was shaking so hard she couldn't unrope. All she could think about was her warm sleeping bag. Looking around for help, she saw her dad was still roped in and also shivering. She tried to open her mouth, but her lips were quivering, and she didn't know what to say.

Tim took one glance in their direction and called out, "We need some help over here. It looks like Sarah and her dad have hypothermia. Gabe, Bobby, and Laura, help me move them into the tents. Sam and Wendy, drop what you're doing and help Doug crank up the stoves. We've got to get something hot down these two right away."

Sarah kept shivering and shivering, until suddenly she was inside the tent and felt her wet clothes being pulled off and Laura gently putting a soft, dry top over her head. "You're going to be fine, Sarah."

Sarah lay in her sleeping bag, still shaking, but getting warmer and warmer as she drifted off to sleep. Then Wendy began shaking her. "Sit up, Sarah. You've got to drink something hot."

"No, no," Sarah said, moving her head back and forth, refusing to open her eyes. "Let me sleep."

"Come on, Sarah. You've got to drink this hot broth. You're hypothermic. You could die if you don't drink." Finally, Wendy and Tim pulled her up and, holding the cup to Sarah's lips, forced her to take little sips. Sarah kept shaking her head and trying to lie down, but Wendy and Tim wouldn't stop until she had drunk the whole cupful. She kept on shaking, so they brought her stew. After she had taken a few bites, they let her lie back down, and she fell asleep, her body finally at rest. In her dreams she heard pounding and shoveling, and tired bodies working against the wind.

Sarah didn't come out for dinner, but from somewhere she heard Doug's voice. "Get some rest and stay warm, folks. Sleep is all important, especially in this higher altitude. It will help with the adjustment. Just keep breathing as normally as possible, and each day will seem easier. Let's hope our hypothermic buddies are recovering in their sleep."

Sarah felt her eyelids close again. Sleep. She could sleep forever, warm at last.

Later, when Sarah finally awoke, there was an eerie silence. Where was the wind? What time was it? She sat up. Wendy and Laura were sleeping on either side of her. Where was her dad? Was he all right? She tried to move to the door, but couldn't get up out of her sleeping bag. No, she had to trust that he was all right. they would have let her know. She had to trust Tim and Doug.

Shivering, Sarah pulled out her journal and snuggled into her warm bag. It was still so cold. Flipping through it, she glanced at the quotes her mother had written at the top of pages throughout the book. Then she opened to one page.

"When a great adventure is offered, you don't refuse it."

—Amelia Earhart

79

Sarah picked up her pen and began writing.

DAY 8—A great adventure it is, but it's hard. I never expected the journey to be so hard.

She gave an involuntary shudder as she thought of yesterday's ordeal. It had come on so suddenly.

I never expected to be this cold, hungry, and scared. I couldn't think. All was a blur. I was out of control, but still I love this climb. I'm making it. I'm climbing Denali and I'm not going to stop.

Sarah read over the quote again. Her dad hadn't actually offered this great adventure. She had to beg him to bring her along. But she was here and nobody would send her back now, unless she chose to go.

Anxious to know if they would climb today, Sarah forced her body over to the tent door and unzipped it, looking out. The weather was horrible: no visibility, no sunshine—no climbing.

Sarah pulled back into the tent and took out the baby wipes. It had been a couple of days since she had freshened up—Sarah, who never missed her morning shower until Mayurvik. She dug through her pack and pulled out a comb, then covered up her dirty hair with her hat. She might not look like a goddess on the outside, but on the inside a goddess she would have to be to complete this journey, whether they climbed today or not.

The goddesses—Artemis, Aphrodite, Athena, Demeter, Hera, Hestia—came flooding through her mind.

Wendy was awake. "Good morning, Amazon." Sarah greeted Wendy more warmly than she ever had.

"Hello," Wendy said, staring at Sarah. "You look better now, but you gave us quite a scare last night."

"I know," Sarah said, whispering. "I was scared too. But I'm all right now—really. Thanks for taking care of me."

"What's the climbing forecast?"

"Zero, zero, zero, I'm afraid."

"Oh, dear. Well, I guess it'll give this old body more time to rest." Sarah was frowning as Wendy patted her arm. "Let's not dwell on it. Amazon, you called me?"

"Yes, you are like the strong warrior woman." Sarah was sure that Wendy pulled back her shoulders when Sarah said it.

"What will you call me, Sarah?" Laura asked in a sleepy voice.

"Medial, the wise woman. So calm and serene, like you've been on this mountain before." Laura raised her eyebrows, her half-opened eyes mysterious.

"You're not surprised I'm talking like this so early in the morning?"

Wendy shook her head. "Hand me that comb. If you're going to call me a goddess, I guess I'd better try to look like one, if that's possible." They all laughed. "I've always enjoyed reading about mythology, especially the goddesses. I even brought a book along about it."

"Really? I do too, ever since my creative writing class two years ago in Eugene. Maybe I could borrow your book later." Sarah kept talking, ignoring the hunger pangs in her stomach. "Our teacher had us doing all sorts of reading about mythology. She told us about the feminine and masculine poles and how we need all poles represented in us to become a complete person, although one pole was often stronger.''

Suddenly Sarah stopped and looked at Laura and Wendy. "Here we are, three women together on Denali, and we've seen so few other women climbing. Can I call myself a woman?''

Laura said softly, "You bet.''

"I'm so glad you're on the same expedition with me. I don't think I could have done it if I were the only female with all these male jocks for company." The three of them laughed, then Sarah inhaled sharply. An image of her mother flooded across her mind. "I haven't really been fair to her.''

"Who?'' asked Laura. "Your mother?''

"How did you know?''

"Goddesses, our mothers, they are all part of us.''

Sam called from outside the tent, and the mood was broken. The three women smiled at one another, and then Wendy called out, "Come into our sanctuary, Sam.''

As he entered, Sam was smiling as usual. "If you three don't get cracking, you're going to miss breakfast. Besides, this young lady and I are long overdue for our chess lesson.''

Her dad had always wanted to teach Sarah how to play. She knew she was smart enough, but the game—and the thought of her dad as instructor—had always scared her. "You're on. But first how about that breakfast you mentioned? By the way, who did my dad sleep with last night?" The others laughed and Sarah felt herself flush. "I mean— Oh, stop it. Where is my dad? And how did you two end up in here?''

"Bobby and I took care of your dad last night and Wendy and Laura took care of you. You both look terrific now. In fact, your dad is feeling so well that he's stripping the socks off Bobby and Doug in poker."

"Well, I hope not. We can't afford to have any more cases of hypothermia."

Sam guffawed loudly, then added, "Your dad checked on you earlier, but Sleeping Beauty and her stepsisters had not awakened yet." Wendy punched Sam and he started to wrestle her on the ground.

Sam changed Sarah's mind about chess. He was a good teacher, quietly letting her take as much time as she needed to figure things out. By lunchtime, Sarah was enjoying herself even though the weather remained the same.

Before dinner, her dad stopped by the tent. "We both had a scare yesterday."

"I know," Sarah said, looking at her dad. "We're lucky the others took care of us. Isn't it funny it hit us both at the same time?"

"Maybe it's in the genes." They both laughed. But then her dad asked in a hurt voice, "Why didn't you tell me you wanted to play chess?"

"Dad, I thought you were busy playing poker all day."

"But I have offered for years to teach you how to play chess."

"I know. I guess I wasn't ready until now."

chapter 10

ALTHOUGH the next morning, Day 9, wasn't sunny, the fog had cleared enough that Doug announced they would push on to 11. Anxious to test out the high altitude, the group dismantled camp in speedy fashion. They were pros now, thought Sarah. Amazing what a few days' practice could do.

Things were always easier for Sarah when she knew what to expect. Change was hard for her, but not for her mother or dad or Mike, who especially thrived on change. Even Gretchen did. She always used to say she was bored if she kept doing the same gymnastic routine over and over.

Sarah liked doing something over and over until she knew it perfectly. Maybe that's why she liked running so much, because it was predictable. At least the training runs were. And now climbing was beginning to feel the same way. Her body was starting to work in sync with her mind because of the practice and routine.

Doug told Sarah that it would be the last day for Walkmans. "Too distracting after this. You'll need all your concentration focused on the climb."

So today Sarah enjoyed her final three hours of climbing to the strains of Paula Abdul and Hammer. She had hardly used her Walkman on this trip, but today she needed to be alone. The bad weather days always made her feel antsy.

Sarah had worried she might feel lonely on the trip, yet she actually felt less lonely than she ever had. Sam, Wendy, Laura, Tim, and now Gabe were becoming her friends. And her dad was always there, whether they were getting along or not. She knew that if she were going to make it to the summit and complete the journey she would have to depend on herself most of all. The thought was scary; however, a year in Mayurvik had taught her self-reliance. Even in Eugene, she had had only one true friend—Gretchen.

Sarah thought back to that Saturday afternoon last month when she had slammed the front door on her mother, who sat drinking tea and grading papers. Sarah had walked out onto the tundra, the wide open space behind their house where the hills went on forever. She wanted to start running, away from the village, out of this world, to the top of McKinley. How she had wished that day she was already climbing.

The snow had finally melted from the tundra. Hiking along, her pack on her back, Sarah had wanted to look up at the huge blue sky uncluttered with tall buildings and dirty air. But she knew if she weren't careful, the bumpy, squishy tundra clumps, with their spring colors of brown and green, would trip her up, and she would twist her ankle. There would go the climb to the summit and her hope of racing competitively next year.

The mossy green tundra was so peaceful and clean

compared to the road down below, where the winter's litterings were strewn about. Beyond the road, the river had looked soft and mushy. Breakup could come any day. Maybe on prom night. If it did, Jack had said, they would all rush out in their formal clothes and watch the Kuskokwim River crash and rumble its way to the Bering Sea, leaving its frozen ice chunks behind.

If only she fit in. Her mother made it sound so simple. "Be yourself, and people will come to respect you."

That day she had missed Oregon more than ever. If only her parents hadn't divorced. If only her mother hadn't met Mike last year. Then Sarah could be living in Eugene, hanging out with Gretchen, running on the school team, and just being one of the honor students at South Eugene High.

Yet sometimes she felt so free in Mayurvik, driving their small boat downriver with Mike to fish for salmon, picking berries on the tundra with her mother, walking on the muddy road to the post office every day to check for a letter from her dad. And most especially walking to school on a March morning watching the gorgeous pink and purple sunrise.

At first, she was the new girl and they all knocked themselves out to be friendly. The girls gossiped with her, and the boys flirted. But after the initial excitement of the first month, Sarah ended up an outsider. Most of the girls thought she was out to get their guys, and the guys were trying to make their girls jealous. Sarah just wanted to have a friend.

As the year went on she felt their silence and withdrew even more. The village kids communicated with one another in such secret ways. Sarah was used to being around noisy people and prided herself on the fact that she was the reserved one. And yet in Mayurvik there was so much nonverbal communication that she didn't pick up on.

From the beginning, Sarah could see that Jack really cared about school. Since the school was so small, with only thirty high school students, chemistry was offered as an independent study course every two years. Sarah, Jack, Michael Andrews, and Anna Pete were the only four taking it, so they were thrown together every day. In February, she saw *Sarah + Jack* printed on Anna's notebook and it made her smile. But until he asked her to the prom, they'd never really done anything together outside of school. Sarah was sad now that she'd let that opportunity for friendship go by.

Sarah's attempts to fit in weren't helped by the fact that Mike was the principal and her mother the English teacher. Deep down, Sarah knew that if Mike hadn't loved Alaska so much, her mother would have stayed in Eugene, if only for Sarah's sake. But now her mother had fallen in love with the Yup'ik Eskimo culture, and she was learning beadwork and studying Yup'ik with one of the teacher aides. She also worried that the students needed more Alaska Native teachers for role models instead of someone like herself.

Two years ago when her mother brought Mike home for dinner after a class at the University of Oregon, Sarah heard the excitement in her mother's voice. She was talking to Mike the way she used to talk to Sarah's dad, long ago before the fights started. After a year of working on his master's in school administration, Mike was dying to get back to Alaska and talked of nothing else.

All along, her mother must have known that if she married Mike, Alaska would come with the package. While Sarah was training for the marathon last summer in San Francisco, her mother and Mike visited Alaska.

Then, in August, when she married Mike, she dragged Sarah into the equation, never considering Sarah's wishes. Her parents were supposed to have shared custody of Sarah, but because her dad traveled so much, he insisted that she couldn't live with him in San Francisco.

Sarah remembered staying out until ten that May night in Mayurvik, just walking the tundra. But her mom and Mike didn't even seem worried when she got back. Mike just glanced up and said, "Sarah, looks like a great summer school program in Fairbanks this summer. We could all take classes, and you could get a head start on your college credits. Plus you could run the Midnight Sun Run, a ten-kilometer race held on June twenty-first, the longest day of the year, at ten o'clock at night—in broad daylight. The whole town comes out, and I bet you'd be running right up front with the top women."

At the water stop, an expedition passed by waving and calling out hello. Two nice-looking guys on a rope team seemed to be checking Sarah out in particular, but she pretended to be adjusting her rope. Young and female, she sensed the extra stares every time she ran into a new group.

As they started climbing again, Sarah thought about the guys. They looked about college age. College. What kind of scholarship could she get graduating from Mayurvik? The University of Alaska Fairbanks had given Jack a scholarship, but Sarah wanted to get as far away from Alaska as possible. Once she had dreamed of a running scholarship. Now she wondered if she'd ever race again.

Gretchen hoped to win a gymnastics scholarship if her senior year went well—crazy Gretchen, who wasn't beautiful, but whose small, taut body was gutsy enough to try any new moves that came along. Guys were always attracted to her; perhaps they thought because she was petite, she needed to be taken care of. Gretchen soon set them straight, but most of them stayed around anyway.

At five feet eight inches, Sarah always felt like a gangly moose around Gretchen—until she met a real moose when driving up the Alaska Highway last summer. Real moose were anything but klutzy. Actually, the only time Sarah didn't feel klutzy was when she was running.

Running—how she had missed it this year. And yet she felt an odd sense of relief not to have the pressure to perform on the tack. Between skiing and basketball and training for this trip, she'd somehow stayed in shape.

Sarah stretched out her arms in the newly emerging sunshine and thought about sunbathing with Gretchen along the Willamette River. She wished Gretchen were on this trip. Gretchen would have kept her laughing and toughened her up. She wouldn't have let Bobby get to her. But Gretchen would never go mountain climbing and risk the chance of an injury that might ruin her future in gymnastics.

Thoughts of the past disappeared quickly when they arrived at 11. She had hardly paid attention to the spot two days ago because of the cold. Now, with the warming sunshine, it seemed somewhat better. But as they set up the tent site, there was little extra room to move around, and all Sarah could think about was that if the snow walls collapsed the tent, spiraling down the mountain she would go . . .

No, no, no, Sarah told herself, as she pounded in the last tent picket. But at lunch the negative thoughts still wouldn't leave her. When they were all gathered to-gether, Bobby announced, "We're halfway up the mountain, folks."

"Not really," Sarah said.

"What's that supposed to mean?"

"Well, we actually started at 7,200 feet, and we still have 11,000 more feet to climb. *And* the hardest part lies ahead."

"Hey, Ms. Pessimist. It's a piece of cake. Haven't you been listening to Tim? He says the groundwork has already been laid." Bobby turned away. "Suit yourself."

Sarah got up and went over to Gabe, who was fooling with his camera again. She'd been interested in photog-raphy ever since a photographer came out to Mayurvik last winter and worked with the high school students.

"Gabe, how do I adjust the light meter to account for the reflection off the snow?" It was confusing talking to Gabe about her life in Mayurvik, yet there was so much she wanted to ask him, and not just about photography.

Gabe was a good teacher. He didn't talk much, just went about his business while Sarah observed, the way the elders taught the young in Mayurvik. Then he gave Sarah the camera. She focused to her right and took a picture of the West Buttress ridge. Then she took a picture in the direction of Kahiltna Base Camp, where the rolling glacier was surrounded by the peaks of Mount Foraker and Mount Hunter. Finally, she turned to her left and took a shot of the long snow ridge with the huge crack running through camp and Kahiltna Dome at the top.

As she tried to capture the immense beauty on film, she appreciated the view even more. Gabe patiently an-swered her questions about taking pictures, unlike her dad, who would have been telling her how much the camera cost in between lectures on light meters and lens action.

Handing the camera back to Gabe, Sarah breathed in deeply and tried to clear her brain of all her negative thoughts about her dad, Bobby, her safety on the mountain. She wanted the expansive beauty of this place to make its way into her soul. Here, away from the frustrations of her old life, she couldn't keep harping on old or new worries. This world was too special and it asked only for the best of Sarah.

chapter 11

SARAH'S head was pounding and she was cold again, so cold. Day 10. Breathing was getting harder and it took more work just to move. But looking out the tent, she smiled. The day was clear. At breakfast she tried to cheer herself up by announcing, "Gang, I've just decided that I've had enough of this cold and I'm heading south, never stopping until I hit the Southern California beaches, where I will lie in the hot sand, my body relaxed and sweating. Anybody want to join me?"

"Sure. I could go for seeing some girls in bikinis," Bobby said.

Sam said. "I'm in. I've always wanted to learn how to surf." Sarah started laughing. She could certainly picture Bobby ogling the beach babes, but not Sam on a surfboard. Doug did not think it was funny.

"Come on, folks. Let's get moving. There's action today. We're heading up to Windy Corner at 13,400 feet. It could be the worst weather on the mountain, if a storm hits, so be prepared.''

They would have to leave their snowshoes behind today and climb with crampons the rest of the trip. With snowshoes, the going had been slow but steady, and Sarah would miss the secure feeling they gave her.

After breakfast everyone spent a few minutes getting accustomed to the crampons. Doug called out, ''Remember folks, for maximum efficiency and safety with these things, you've got to keep all three points on the snow.''

Sarah picked one up and walked it along the ground. Like a giant insect, its legs attacked the snow. ''June Bugs, here we come,'' she called out. As she fitted the crampons on her climbing boots, Sarah told herself that was how she would look at them—giant insects on her feet attaching to the snow and keeping her safe. Laura and Wendy started laughing as Sarah raised her arms and made monster noises.

She walked past her dad and waved. Then she heard a hissing sound. Turning around, Sarah found her father sprawled on the snow and ran over to help him.

''Don't laugh. Don't say a word,'' her dad said as he sat up.

''Dad. Give me a little credit. I just wanted to see if you were all right.'' Sarah offered her dad an arm up, but he shook is head.

''Of course, I'm all right.''

''What happened?''

''Like a stupid idiot, I tripped, and one foot landed on the other. I guess a crampon punctured the rubber on the other boot.''

Tim came over with a repair kit and quickly applied a rubber patch to stop the leak. Sarah knew that if too much air leaked out, the boot's insulation would be lost.

As she watched Tim kneeling down beside her father, fixing his boot, she thought her dad looked like a little kid being dressed by his mother. Funny, she'd never thought of her dad as young before. When Tim was finished, Sarah tried to sneak away.

"Sarah?"

She turned back around.

"It could have happened to anyone, you know."

"I know. This snow is pretty slippery."

"You're the one who's been getting careless, walking around with your Walkman and taking photographs. This trip is hard work."

"Very hard work. But I also thought it was supposed to be something fun we did together. Instead, all you do is lecture me about—"

"Sarah? Could you give me a hand with my sled over here?"

"Be right there, Laura," Sarah said, glaring at her dad. She turned to go, trying to swallow her anger, but couldn't resist mumbling, "You're the one who tripped, not me."

Sarah went over and started helping Laura load her sled. "Don't let him get to you. You're doing a great job on this trip, keeping up and carrying your own weight. I never could have done it at your age."

Watching Laura's sure, small movements, Sarah didn't know how to help. "Every time he opens his mouth he has to criticize me. He's always treated me like a little kid. Now it's only getting worse."

"I don't think so. I think this trip is forcing him to see you in another light. And it's hard. You're growing up. You're not just his daughter now, but an important member of this team. Imagine having a daughter tough enough to climb Denali at age seventeen." Laura paused to look over at Sarah's dad. "That's a lot of pressure for him. Maybe he'll find out you're stronger than he is.''

Working on the sled helped calm Sarah down, as did Laura's words. "Laura, your down parka is sticking out over here. We'd better strap it in better." Laura pulled out one of her extra bungie cords, and Sarah helped her secure it tightly over the top of the load and then hook it onto the other side. "There, that ought to do it."

"Thanks, Sarah. You're really getting good at this. I bet you'd make a great guide someday." Sarah couldn't help but smile. A Denali guide? She wished her dad believed in her the same way Laura did.

When they finally started climbing, Sarah began to feel better. The warm sun and exercise helped her feet and hands thaw out. She began to think about what Laura had said. Maybe she was growing up and it made her dad feel old.

Then her mind turned to happier thoughts. She had probably just climbed past 11,240 feet, the altitude of Mount Hood and higher up than she had ever climbed before. Sarah's heart pumped with excitement. She was really going to do it. She was climbing higher and higher and getting stronger and stronger.

Actually, the climb to the plateau at 12,200 feet went slowly because they weren't used to the crampons. But Sarah didn't mind because it gave her plenty of time to view the spectacular vista. Peter Glacier, a rough surface of craggy points and patches of blue ice, lay on one side and the sprawling white tundra on the other. Down below, the gray mountains grew smaller and smaller as the team climbed upward into the big white wilderness.

Sarah was enjoying herself until she started hearing eerie sounds in the background—an echo followed by a whooshing sound. "What's that?" she called ahead to Doug.

Doug yelled back in his booming voice. "Didn't you hear my announcement? We're coming into major avalanche country, right around 12,000 feet. You'll see them all around you. First person to hear one before we see it gets seconds on dessert tonight."

"How come I haven't heard them before?" Sarah wondered aloud.

"Oh, there have been smaller avalanche rumblings the whole trip, but nothing like this."

Sarah didn't want to hear another. And she certainly didn't want to see one. She thought about Doug's avalanche lesson on the first day. "Stay away from walls, cliffs, and overhangs." That she would do. She took a few deep breaths and began to fall into the rhythm of their climbing again. Then out of the blue up ahead Sarah heard a shout.

"Help. Grab it. Grab it." Everybody stopped along the line. Tumbling quickly by, too fast for Sarah to try and grab it with her ice ax, was a parka. She planted her poles, and turned slowly around, just in time to watch the parka plummet off the plateau, down into Peter Glacier.

Immediately the three rope teams stopped for a break. Sarah listened in terror as Laura explained that she had slipped on her crampons, taking a bad fall. Her sled overturned, causing her coat to jar loose and take off down the mountain.

"Too late now," Doug said. "If the parka had been strapped in properly, Laura, this wouldn't have happened. I don't know how many times I have to tell you to check your loads to make sure they're secure." Doug pulled his water bottle out of the side pocket of his backpack and took a long swig.

"Doug, I'm also to blame. I helped Laura pack her sled."

Laura shook her head and said, "No, that's not what happened. I redid—"

"You know, I really don't care what happened. I just want you all to follow the safety rules. Enough of this." Doug waved his arm at Laura and Sarah as if to dismiss them. "Everybody take some liquid refreshment and then let's get this show back on the road. I guess we should be grateful that someone wasn't hurt or a life lost. But we haven't any extra parkas. You'll have to make do."

Sarah looked over at Laura's ashen-colored face and was filled with anger. Laura wasn't crying, but she looked scared to death, and Doug couldn't seem to care less. Laura could be badly hurt, and all Doug cared about was that stupid old parka.

As the others drank water or Tang, Tim took Laura aside. Sarah wanted to go over, but she felt that Laura needed to be alone right now. She noticed Tim roped in behind Laura when they started climbing again. Sarah felt her climbing rhythm was destroyed as she struggled up the 500-foot Squirrel Hill. All she wanted to do was quit for the day and get out of avalanche country.

When they finally stopped for lunch, Sarah went right over to Laura. "How are you? Was it a bad fall?"

"I'm fine. A little bruised and rattled, that's all."

"I feel terrible, Laura. I thought we had secured your load so nothing could fall out."

Laura smiled. "Didn't you hear me try to explain to Doug? It's not your fault, Sarah. After you helped me, I kept fiddling around with it and tried to cram the coat in. It was so dumb. I don't know why I did it."

"Hey, we've all done dumb things." Sarah hugged her friend, something she usually didn't feel comfort-

97

able doing. "And look how far we've come with every-body still strong and healthy. That's what really matters."

"You're right. But seeing my parka fall off the mountain made me feel like I was going with it."

After lunch Sarah noticed Doug standing perfectly still, staring up the mountain. Then he began writing something down. Though she was still angry that he hadn't shown Laura more concern, curiosity won out. "Doug, what are you doing?"

"Sketching out the afternoon's climb on paper," he said without looking up.

"Why? I've never seen you do that before." Sarah moved closer to see what he was drawing.

"I've climbed Denali almost a dozen times, but this section can be so confusing and dangerous. If I sketch out the trouble spots from this vantage point, while the visibility is good, I'll know which route to take, even if the weather turns nasty."

Sarah felt her stomach tighten up again, the way it did this morning over Laura's incident. Doug kept marking out the positions of crevasses and questionable spots he could see as he studied the mountain and de-cided the route they would take. And Sarah kept stand-ing next to him, watching the mountain.

Doug tried to relax the group before started climbing again, as if to apologize for this morning's outburst. "Well, no takers yet on advance warning of avalanches. I've been hearing lots of noises myself. Guess I'll get all the extra dessert myself tonight."

"I don't know, Doug. You'd better let me have it. Don't you need to be watching your figure?" Sam said. Bobby and Wendy started making pig noises, while the others laughed. Sam always got more laughs than Doug.

"Seriously folks, it could take us quite a while to

reach Windy Corner at 13–4. So take it slow and steady, and save some energy for the end.''

Sarah started out fine, trudging along like Artemis on a great journey. But during the last two hours—why did something always happen the last two hours?—a whiteout developed. Suddenly her fellow climbers were swallowed up in a fog and Sarah could see only a few feet ahead. Voices seemed to reverberate and bounce off imaginary walls. Her head was pounding, and she couldn't concentrate.

Sarah figured that by now Doug had only the orange wands and his notes to help him determine their route. She hated this. She wanted to go home. Why had she ever come on this trip anyway?

The wind was so strong that as soon as the powdery snow fell it immediately blew away. Sarah found herself climbing on sheer ice. She had to plant her crampons even more carefully at every step, using her ice ax for extra balance. Sarah would have loved some music right now, but she needed to focus all her concentration on the climbing, or else she could slip down, down, down, down into Peter Glacier.

To fight the wind, she put on her heavy down parka and pulled the fur ruff on the hood up around her face, burying her head down in her neck. She couldn't see anyway, so if she just pointed herself ahead, and imagined the course in her mind, she would be all right. She pretended she was blind, that she had to live by her other senses. But then she started to feel a little crazy. What if she really were blind? What if she never saw this beautiful world again?

Suddenly Tim's words came pounding through her brain. ''The real climbing begins after 11. The real climbing begins after 11.'' The real climbing started higher than she'd ever been before. Yes, I want to be a real climber. Yes, I want to be a real climber, Sarah kept repeating to herself.

But her hands were freezing. She just couldn't get them warm today. She had three layers on her hands—polypropylene liners, wool mittens, and nylon overmitts—and still they felt numb. She tried moving them around, but she couldn't feel them. All she could hope was that they weren't frostbitten. She wanted to stop and put them under her armpits to see if her body heat would help warm them, but she had to keep climbing. That was the only way she would make it.

When they finally arrived at 13,400 feet—Windy Corner—it was ten below, but the wind had stopped, and the storm thankfully was over for now. Sarah's body was shaking as she looked around in wonder. She had made it through the awful afternoon. And now it was so warm and beautiful.

Sarah took her pack off, her arms and legs weak with fatigue. Thirsty, she finally managed to get her water bottle out and took a long drink.

Tim came over. "How are you holding up?"

"Oh God, am I glad we stopped. I felt like I wasn't going to make it. I couldn't see, and I got so cold and scared." Sarah felt as though she was going to cry, but her tears might freeze. She couldn't keep falling apart—it wasn't good for the others.

"It was bad, so don't get down on yourself. You're holding up just fine. About five of our climbers a year give up before 14 and head back to base camp. They just can't hack it. But not you. And look around. It's warming up. This crazy mountain changes the weather every few minutes, whenever it feels like it. That's why they call it The Weathermaker."

Sarah's head was throbbing and her legs were about to buckle, so she unroped and sat down next to Sam and

Laura, who both said they felt weak and nauseous—the first signs of altitude sickness. She didn't know if her headache was from altitude sickness, the cold, or just the afternoon's demanding climb. Right now she didn't care. She lay down on a pad and closed her eyes. All she wanted to do was sleep.

As if through an echo chamber, she heard Doug's voice. "We're lucky, folks. The weather's not too bad here right now, so let's set up camp right over there. I was hoping to make it all the way to 14, but we've pushed hard enough. We'd never chance this place for two nights because it's too unsheltered from the wind, but for tonight it'll have to do."

Then Sarah was startled to hear her dad's voice right by her ear. "Sarah, I'll set up the tent. You just keep resting."

She started to get up. "No, no, I can help."

"You look awful. Please just take it easy. I'll get the tent up as soon as I can, so you can rest before dinner. You've been working so hard."

"So have you, Dad," she murmured before she closed her eyes again.

Then, what seemed like only moments later, Sarah awoke to screaming. "Move away from that overhang! Now! It's an avalanche and another could come any second. Move!" Sarah sat up to see Sam sprawled on the ground. As Sam struggled to his feet, Doug kept yelling "Move, move." Yet Sam seemed stuck in slow motion, his arms flailing, legs slipping beneath him, as snow kept coming down. Finally, he stood up straight. The snow had stopped.

Like scared children, the group huddled around Doug. Sarah's dad walked with Sam, his arm around Sam's shoulder. While Doug lectured, Sam stood with his eyes downcast and shoulders slumped.

"We've repeatedly warned you to stay away from walls, cliffs, and overhangs, and never to put packs near them. You've got to stay out in the wide open spaces because anything can happen."

"I just brought my pack over and stopped to catch my breath. I'm not feeling very well. Then I heard this noise . . ." Sam's voice broke off. After a pause, he spoke again. "It was incredibly stupid. I won't do it again."

"Like I said, the mountain doesn't give second chances. You've all been so careful lately, until today. But after Laura's sled incident and now this, I don't know what to think. Don't blow it because you're so tired." Doug walked away, then stopped. "As far as avalanches go, that was a tiny one. We were very lucky. Get out the shovels. We've got some clearing off to do."

By the time the mounds of snow were shoveled and the campsite was set up, Sarah was so exhausted she could hardly move. Later, she tossed and turned as she dreamt of avalanches during a two-hour nap. She felt well enough to get up for dinner. But she still seemed suspended outside the group.

In the murmur of conversation, her dad asked, "What's that mountain over there?"

"Oh, that's McKinley's Child, aka Mount Hunter. And the bigger one next to it is called McKinley's Woman. That may not make you ladies too happy. I guess you could say those old-timers weren't too liberated." Doug laughed heartily, and Sarah's dad joined in.

"Let's just call it Mount Foraker, its rightful name," Gabe said. Wendy gave Gabe an approving hug, and everyone else applauded, except Laura, who got that faraway look in her eyes again. Even Bobby seemed to agree, pumping Sarah on the back. Funny, thought Sarah, Bobby's a hard guy to figure out. I would have taken him for a male chauvinist pig all the way.

12

REACHING 14,000 feet would be a big milestone, Sarah thought when she woke up the next morning. There was a park ranger at 14. Somehow that sounded safer, more civilized. Sarah took out her journal and wrote.

> DAY 11—This is it. I'll be joining Ray Genet and thousands of climbers through the years who have made it to 14. Tim said that anyone who makes it to 14 should be very proud. That everything after 14 is icing on the cake. Well, I'm ready for some dessert. I've had plenty of the freeze-dried entrées.

Sarah turned to the next page, and there in her mother's handwriting was Eleanor Roosevelt's quote:

> *"You must do the thing you think you can-*
> *not do."*

She continued to write.

Boy, I didn't think I could keep climbing yesterday. If somebody had offered me a one-way ticket off this mountain and over to Hawaii, I would have been gone in a flash. But like so often happens after some food and sleep, the day always gets better.

Sarah put away the journal when Sam started rustling around. She wondered what she would have to do today that she didn't want to do.

As Sarah took a bite of her bagel with peanut butter at breakfast, Bobby came up and said, "You like to hold grudges, don't you?"

Sarah wanted to concentrate on her climb to 14 today, not argue with Bobby. What is his problem? she wondered, as she swallowed her food. He'd seemed so normal last night.

"You've avoided me since that stupid tent deal." Sarah shrugged her shoulders.

"You ice-maiden types make me sick. Give a guy a break once in a while. Now your dad, there's somebody who knows how to have a good time." With that, Bobby walked away.

She gritted her teeth and mumbled to herself, "What a jerk."

Laura walked over and said, "Don't let him get to

you. That's what he wants. You need to save your energy for more important things.'' Laura took a spoonful of oatmeal and leaned in closer to Sarah. ''He really does have a good side. Like last night when he hugged me and said. 'Thank God it wasn't you that fell off the mountain.' ''

Sarah shook her head.

''Besides, I think he has a crush on you.''

Doug interrupted the breakfast conversation. ''Let's hit it, folks. Back and forth to 14 the next two days, and then a couple of days off to really enjoy the sunshine at 14 and get used to the altitude. Remember, everything gets tougher from here on out. You've got to keep drinking lots of fluids, eating even when you don't feel like it. You'll be pushing beyond what you think is your limit. So take it slow and stop when you need to.''

Just my luck, Sarah thought, as she roped in behind Bobby with Doug in the lead. As they began climbing, the snow was six inches deep. Sarah longed for her snowshoes, but an hour later when the wind picked up and the terrain turned icy, she was glad for her crampons.

How ridiculous to think that Bobby had a crush on her. Since they'd started climbing, Bobby already had yelled back at her twice. And now his constant whistling was rattling her nerves. How his silly whistle could pierce the air so well, she couldn't figure out. But it looked like the fog might be settling in. Maybe that would muffle his noise.

Sarah hated this weather. Anything could go wrong. Yesterday they were lucky. They only lost Laura's parka, not Laura. And Sam's avalanche was only a tiny one. Every day so far they had been lucky. But today or tomorrow someone might get so sick or hypothermic that they would all have to stop until the person got better, or worse, turn around and go down the mountain.

Sarah just wanted to safely reach the sunny, wide open spaces of the Genet Basin at 14. She'd seen pictures of happy climbers sunbathing there—so unlike the pictures at 17,000 feet, where the climbers were always bundled up, a storm swirling around them.

In Talkeetna, Tim had told them the story of Ray Genet, the famous climber who had climbed Denali more times than anyone else. Born in France, he had spent his last twenty years in Alaska climbing The Mountain—Denali. Genet Basin was named after him. But on a climb up Mount Everest he had died of exposure right below the summit.

Sarah had studied the picture of Genet hanging in the Summit pavilion in Talkeetna. With his sunglasses, long black hair pulled back in a ponytail, and his famous red bandanna tied around his head, he looked just like his nickname, "the pirate." Fearless and invincible, he'd seemed immortal.

Tim must have told Genet's story hundreds of times, yet it still seemed to puzzle and sadden him. "Imagine Ray Genet, of all people, dying on a mountain." Shaking his head, he added, "You just never know. You can never be too careful."

Sarah was beginning to feel herself lose control. One minute she felt fine and the next she was almost suffocated by chest pains. She tried to concentrate on her crampons gripping the snow. But she kept thinking of Pete Huddleston, the photographer who had come out to teach a two-week photography residency in Mayurvik last winter. Just last week, while in Anchorage with her dad, Sarah had read in the paper that Pete had died while photographing a rafting trip on the Nenana River. Like Genet, Pete was so alive, so committed to his work. He was the first person to get her interested in photography. Why did people like that have to die so young, doing what they loved? Or was that the best way to die?

Why couldn't her father have been a fisherman? She could be safely battling salmon on the Chulitna River right now, instead of battling this mountain. She shook her head and pulled back her shoulders. Her mind was wandering. She'd worked too hard to get this far. She couldn't let her emotions take over.

Doug stopped for a water break and Sarah gratefully slowed down. She felt tense and anxious, as though something awful was going to happen. Sitting on her pack drinking water and eating an energy bar, she could feel her heart pounding.

"Hi, Sarah. You doing okay?"

"Oh, I'll make it. Thanks, Gabe."

"Same here. It's been a rough go lately. I'm sure looking forward to those rest days."

Sarah let out a relaxed sigh. She'd forgotten the rest days. Soon she'd be safe at 14 and could take it easy. She much preferred the planned rest days to the "unexpected weather" rest days. The thought of rest and relaxation at 14 would keep her going for a couple of more hours.

As they started back up again, Sarah felt refreshed, especially when Doug announced that they should be at Genet Basin in less than an hour.

Suddenly, without warning, Sarah's rope jerked, and she was yanked off her feet and dragged forward, before finally digging her ice ax in the snow and coming to a stop. In that split second she felt her body seize up and her mind go blank. When her brain cleared, Sarah was afraid to sit up. Instead she looked around, stretching out her neck between her body's spasmodic shudders.

Up ahead Bobby had disappeared, and Doug was on the ground too. Then she heard a scream pierce the air and fade down the mountainside. "H-E-L-P!"

"Freeze," Tim yelled from behind. "Everybody plant your axes!"

Doug had been dragged backward about ten feet. Sarah watched Doug stand up, just as Tim reached her side. "Stay right there, Sarah," he said. "You reacted perfectly." Tim squeezed Sarah's shaking arm and gave her a reassuring smile. Then he took a couple of snow pickets off his pack and anchored them in the ground. He wrapped the slack rope at the end of Sarah's line around her ice ax and the snow pickets. At the same time, Doug wrapped the loose rope in front of him around his ice ax. Then Doug got up and took off his pack and started digging a hole.

Sarah watched all this, her body paralyzed except for her lungs, which were panting hard. She felt as if she were holding on for dear life—that any minute another one of them would disappear into the snow without a trace. Oh, my God, this is it. My luck has run out. Suddenly the snow beneath her, which she had cursed and moaned about, was her only thread to survival.

"Where is Bobby?" What is happening?" Sarah's throat had tightened so much that she was surprised any sound came out.

"Bobby's fallen into a crevasse just up ahead. But it's going to be all right. You acted quickly enough to stop his fall and prevent yourself and Doug from getting pulled in with him. You are really something," Tim said.

How could Bobby be there one minute and gone the next? Was this some bad dream?

"What am I supposed to do now?" Sarah's voice sounded so froggy and foreign to her ears. She wanted to help Bobby, but she was so scared. She could be sucked in next and then her dad, Laura, Sam, Wendy, Gabe . . . "Can we get him out, Tim?" Can we please get out of here? she prayed.

"What am I supposed to do next, Tim?" Sarah felt as if she were screaming.

"Just lie there, let your weight sink into the ground." But I might sink through the earth, Sarah wanted to cry. "We just need your weight here anchoring him. Think how much pressure his weight and equipment have created." Tim kept talking as he worked, taking off the extra rope around his waist and tying it into Sarah's rope and then wrapping it around the anchors and ice ax several times.

"I don't know how he is yet, but Gabe and Doug are helping him. When he starts climbing out, he's going to be pulling hard, so just stay anchored." And pray, Sarah thought, as Gabe moved carefully past her, poking holes in the snow with his ice ax. Oh God, maybe there are more crevasses. Roped in to her dad and Laura and moving as carefully as possible, Gabe was belaying out to the edge of the crevasse.

Sarah kept listening for Bobby's voice, but it was strangely silent. Maybe he's already dead, she thought, his face deathly white, like a criminal hanged in the Old West. Sarah closed her eyes and tried to erase the picture. How could she think such thoughts?

She turned her body a bit so that she could watch Gabe as he climbed to the edge of the crevasse and began taking off his gear. He dug holes with a little shovel and placed his ice ax, pack, sled, and snowshoes around the lip of the crevasse, all the while keeping up a conversation with Bobby.

This equipment would prevent Bobby's rope from rubbing and chafing against the hardened snow at the edge of the crevasse. It would also stabilize the edge of the crevasse, so that it didn't break off anymore. If the lip of the crevasse did break off, Bobby wouldn't be able to get out safely.

Even though Sarah was cold and stiff all over, she suddenly felt suspended from the scene, as if she were looking down from the ceiling of a movie theater at an action adventure. She felt distant now, the fear buried under layers of paralyzing fog.

"How are you, Bobby? Are you all right?" Sarah heard Gabe say. "Just keep hanging on. You're doing great. We'll get you moving out of there in just a minute."

Then it was Doug's voice speaking. "Hang on. You can do it." Never had Doug's voice sounded so gentle.

Sarah tried to focus her mind. One moment Bobby was climbing up the mountain, the next, dangling twenty-five feet down a crevasse, struggling for his life. Stories about accidents were one thing. Having the person in front of you disappear into the ice and snow was something else.

It could have been me, Sarah thought. I was right behind Bobby. Or Doug. He was the last one to cross that spot safely just seconds before. Why didn't it give way under him?

Tim answered as if Sarah had spoken her question out loud. "The crevasse must have been covered by hardened snow. The sun, plus our weight, made it give way, just at the moment Bobby climbed by."

"How do you feel, Bobby?" Doug's voice sounded so far away.

"I don't know." Finally, Bobby's voice for the first time, small and scared.

"Try moving your arms and legs."

"I can't . . . I can't move any . . . thing. I just can't

111

do it . . ." His voice broke and then faded away. It sounded as though he was crying. Bobby Snyder was crying.

"Just relax. Let go of the rope if you want. Your harnesses will keep you safe. You're tough, old buddy."

"No . . . I'm afraid. I don't know what happened. I was climbing and then all of a . . ." Bobby sounded so weak.

"Don't talk anymore, Bobby. Save your energy. We'll keep talking to you. You just listen. Don't worry. We're going to get you out of there."

Then Sarah heard Doug speak in a different, questioning voice. "Well, Gabe, who will it be? Me or you?"

"I'd like to go down, Doug. I can handle it."

"I'm sure you can. Go to it. We'll be up here, backing you two up." Sarah could hardly believe it was Doug speaking. He was like a different person. In a real emergency, he had left his tough exterior behind.

Doug motioned to Laura and Sarah's dad, and they made their way out to the crevasse, nodding at Tim and Sarah as they passed by. Meanwhile, Gabe was setting up the ascenders and webbing he would need to pull himself back out. Sarah kept trying to shift her body around, trying to see more. But she knew any extra movement on this snow was dangerous.

When Laura and Sarah's dad were close enough to give Gabe enough rope to belay down into the crevasse, Gabe nodded at Doug and went over the lip and down the crevasse to Bobby, their ropes side by side.

Sarah could barely hear Gabe's voice. "Okay, now, Bobby, we're going to get us both out of here. But first we've got to do some setting up. How are you doing?" Sarah listened for an answer, but heard nothing.

"First I'm going to help you get out of your pack and unclip the sled. . . . Remember, everything's hooked up separately to the rope, so nothing will be lost. . . ."

How could Gabe be so calm, Sarah wondered.

"Okay, now . . . your jumar ascenders are there clipped to the rope right above you."

"I can't see anything. My eyes are watering." At last, Bobby had spoken.

"That's okay. Take your time. Breathe deeply and close your eyes a minute. . . . Ready to try now? Reach up for those ascenders. Got 'em?"

"I think so," came Bobby's answer.

"Good. Now I'm going to attach some webbing to form a dangling stirrup on each ascender." Sarah heard nothing for a while.

"Okay. I've got them set up. Now we've got the two jumars spread out on the rope, one on top of the other. Put your right foot into the lower stirrup. You'll have to bend your knee to get it in. . . ."

"I can't . . . do . . . it."

"Yes, you can. We'll do it together. Just take your time. Start sliding up that rope with your right foot in the stirrup and your right hand on the lower jumar. . . . Stop and rest when you have to. . . . There you go. . . . Good job. . . . Now, we're going to do the same thing with the other leg. . . . I know it's hard. All your weight is on two points. . . . It really kills the arms, doesn't it?"

"I'm . . . so . . . tired. Can't . . . you get . . . me up any . . . other way?" Bobby sounded half dead.

"We could pull you up, if we had to, Bobby. But it would be even harder on you. Trust me. Just keep going," Doug called down.

Slowly Bobby made his way up the rope, moving the jumars inch by inch, with Gabe right beside him, encouraging and directing him. Sarah lay on her pack and prayed the whole time, promising God she wouldn't complain, would get along with her dad, would be friendlier to Bobby, if only he got out safely.

Doug radioed out and let base camp and the medical tent at 14 know about the accident. Two other climbing expeditions passed through and offered to help, but Tim waved them on, saying everything was under control.

For two agonizing hours Bobby pulled his way up the rope. While he was climbing, Sarah, Laura, and Sarah's dad stayed put. Tim set up a stove, and Wendy and Sam made hot drinks and food and laid out a sleeping bag for Bobby. Everyone moved around as little as possible.

Sarah couldn't stop shaking. Sam brought her some hot chocolate. "Here, you've earned this. I think Bobby's moving well enough for you to sit up. This'll make you feel better." Sarah took a long drink. "Quick thinking, kid."

Sarah shook her head. "I wasn't thinking, Sam. I just planted my ax, out of shock and fear, nothing else."

"You did the smart thing."

"He could have died, Sam, and Doug and I could have gone in with him. Or the rest of you could have fallen in more crevasses."

"Yes, but he didn't. And you didn't and the rest of us didn't. He's almost out now and our safety procedures are working. What are you so down about? Like I said, you did the smart thing. Not like me and the avalanche. You don't now how lucky you are," he said, creeping back to the stove.

Sarah lay back down, thinking. She hadn't realized that the avalanche incident had bothered Sam that much. He always laughed everything off, never seemed down or discouraged.

Finally, when Bobby was only a few feet from the

top, Doug waved everyone over and instructed them on how to line up behind one another and pull him out the final feet. For several minutes they all pulled hard on the rope until Bobby came up and over the lip.

Sarah could hear a collective sigh of relief when Bobby was sighted. But he was in bad shape. Shivering uncontrollably, he was white-faced and numb, his arms limp at his sides. When he collapsed right on the ground after unroping, Sarah could feel his pain inside herself, as if the life had been ripped out of both of them.

It wasn't until Tim and Doug got Bobby into the sleeping bag and then dry clothes that Sarah realized how cold she was. Her legs and feet were stiff from lying so long in the same position. Finally unroping and taking off her pack, she forced herself to move around and drink more hot chocolate.

While Tim and Gabe stayed with Bobby, Doug talked to the rest of the group. "We're going to push on to 14 as soon as Bobby is able, probably in thirty minutes or so."

"But Doug." Sarah's dad lowered his voice. "Bobby's just been through hell. Is he really ready to go? We can camp here if need be." The others nodded in agreement.

"No way, John. I just talked to base camp, and it sounds like 13 is fogging up and that weather might be moving on up here. Besides, we're three-quarters of the way between 13 and 14 now and we'll be much better off camping at Genet Basin tonight. Fourteen is clear, and the medical team is ready for Bobby. And at 14 Bobby will be able to rest as many days as he needs to." Doug looked around at the group. "Now that it's settled, I think we'll send a rope team up to 14 to get a tent set up and more hot food going for Bobby. Gabe's volunteered to go, so that means Laura and John, you'll be taking off shortly."

Doug went back over to Bobby, while Sarah and her dad walked over to each other. "You really held your own today, Sarah," her dad said as he gave her a hug. "But as badly as I feel for Bobby, I'm so grateful it wasn't you."

Sarah held back the tears. "It could have been me, but I would have pulled myself out if I had to. I have to believe that. If not, I shouldn't be here," she said, looking over at the crevasse.

Taking Sarah by the shoulders, her dad said, "I know you could have done it. If I didn't, I never would have brought you on this trip. I just would have gone crazy worrying about you down there for two hours."

Sarah looked up at him and felt her voice crack. "Dad, didn't it scare you?"

"Of course. I'm not made of steel, you know." Her dad turned to rope in.

"Dad? I'm glad you spoke up to Doug. We all are worried about Bobby, and you were brave enough to voice it. Good luck climbing. I'll see you soon." Sarah's dad nodded his head and waved as they pulled out.

Bobby looked awful when he crawled out of the sleeping bag, his face still chalky and his shoulders slumped. But at least he wasn't shaking all over. Sarah overhead him say to Doug as they roped in, "I'm scared. I don't know if I can do this."

"Bobby. We don't have to go now. We can wait here as long as you want, and join the others later. Or we can pull you up in a bivouac sack."

"No, I want to stay with the team." His voice sounded so weak, Sarah hardly recognized it. "We've got to stick together. That's the only way we're going to make it. So let's just get this over with."

"Okay." Doug grabbed Bobby around the shoulders. "Then here we go. You'll be fine. If you can get through this afternoon, you can get through anything. And anytime you want to stop, just turn around and wave at Tim."

Sarah had wanted to go up to Bobby, to tell him how brave he was, but there was no opportunity. Doug hustled them along so quickly, and she didn't really want to talk to Bobby in front of everyone.

When they started climbing again, Sarah's breaths began coming in short gasps. She tried to stop but couldn't. Bobby was up in the first team, roped between Doug and Wendy. Sarah kept watching him, worrying, waiting for something else to happen.

Finally, a few minutes later, Sarah's breathing settled down and her mind cleared. As they approached 14,000 feet they climbed east along the West Buttress, trying to stay above the heavily crevassed ice field below. Sarah wondered if everyone's heart was pounding as hard as hers.

Suddenly the climbing became easier, even though she found it harder to breathe. I've made it this far, thought Sarah. It doesn't matter how much farther I, Bobby, or any of us goes. I've made it over halfway and I haven't given up. I survived a crevasse accident; we all have. No matter what else happens, I've got this to hold on to.

The sun was shining brightly overhead, and Sarah hadn't seen such wide, open land since base camp. It was like heaven in wintertime. Then as if it were a sign, there appeared Denali way in the distance, like a candy mountain jutting into the sky. As they climbed into the camp at 14, Sarah knew everybody was smiling, even Bobby. They were greeted with applause and cheers by Laura, Gabe, her dad, and other climbers who had heard the news of Bobby's accident.

Sam fell down on his knees and shouted, "Hallelujah!" Then he jumped back up, and he and Wendy started singing, "Hallelujah, come on get happy. We're going to chase all the blues away . . ."

This time Sarah joined in, her croaky, off-key voice balanced by her enthusiasm and joy. She'd always longed for her mother's clear soprano voice, and usually didn't sing out loud in public. But today she sang her own song. Nobody was listening anyway, and even if they were, they couldn't take away her happiness.

ALL night Sarah tossed and turned, haunted by Bobby's face—Bobby dangling down in the crevasse, Bobby crying out for help, Bobby finally letting go. Then the dream changed. Suddenly it was Sarah hanging over the crevasse, screaming in agony, dropping down . . . down . . . down.

They would have to climb back to 11 today, Day 12, for the supplies. They would have to pass Bobby's crevasse. Sarah vaguely remembered her dad talking to her in the middle of the night. If she didn't hurry along now, he'd be in here dragging her out for breakfast. Getting dressed quickly, she stood outside the tent in the already bright sunlight. She needed a moment to herself to summon up her courage. Courage. That's what Bobby had yesterday.

Fixing her favorite breakfast of instant oatmeal, she talked quietly with Gabe and Wendy, but kept looking over at Bobby, who was talking to Tim. His eyes were scared, like the little kid who got beaten up by the bully at school and kept expecting it to happen again.

"Announcement time." Doug seemed his old self today, although everyone else was subdued. He didn't even have to quiet the group down to get their attention. "Looks like a good day for relaxing in the sunshine, folks. Air out those damp clothes and sleeping bags and have some fun." Doug shook his hips and clapped his hands until he got people smiling.

"We don't need to drag everybody back down to 11 with us because we're carrying fewer supplies now. Tim and I are going down and John here has volunteered. Gabe's going to stay up with the rest of you, and is offering free photography lessons." Sarah nodded her head at her dad and smiled. He never could resist an added challenge. "That should do it unless somebody else wants to come along for the ride."

Sarah felt the tension release from her body. She could stay put for a day. Do nothing. Be by herself. She expected Wendy or somebody else to volunteer to go down, but the meeting ended quietly. "We should be back at the end of the day."

Sarah's dad walked over to her as she poured herself another cup of herbal tea. "You were laughing at me." But he didn't sound angry.

"No, I wasn't. I finally figured out that you're really a guide in training, just like Gabe. Maybe you'll be the one who ends up living in Alaska," Sarah said, giving her dad a poke in the arm. "Actually, I'm thrilled not to be moving today."

"Yesterday was tough. For all of us. I see Bobby's already gone back into the tent to rest. I guess he had a rough night. He really strained the muscles in his arms yesterday, pulling himself out of the crevasse."

120

Sarah's dad studied her face. "You had a pretty rough time yourself last night."

"Don't remind me." Sarah yawned. "You know, a nap sounds like a great idea. Have a safe trip."

Later Sarah woke up confused. By now the days and nights were so muddled she had no idea what time it was. Journal writing and then back to Catherine and Heathcliff.

DAY 12—rest day at 14,000 feet.

I don't want to think about Bobby's accident anymore. Have to put it behind me. I did the right thing, but I don't know how or why. I thought important things were planned and practiced in this life. I did it just by instinct or utter fear.

Sarah started shivering and flipped through the pages to find another of her mother's quotes.

"*Some trees grow very tall and straight and large in the forest close to each other, but some must stand by themselves or they won't grow at all.*"

—Oliver Wendell Holmes

Why am I always the different one? Will I always need to stand alone to find my *way? Who else would be crazy enough to climb Denali at my age?*

Nature called and on her way back from the "elegant" latrine with the wooden seat, Sarah noticed a group of four climbers eating lunch in the bright sunshine. They waved her over.

"Allo. How are you?" Sarah loved their accents. French maybe, or Swiss.

"Good. I think." With his black hair and red bandanna, one of the climbers reminded Sarah of Genet. "Are you French?"

"Oui, oui." They all nodded, smiling. Sarah was pleased she had guessed correctly. She thought those were French flags on their packs.

Then a blond man with his hair pulled back in a ponytail spoke. *"Parlez-vous français?"*

"No, no. I wish I did, but I've been living out in the bush and they don't have French classes."

"Pardon?"

"I'm sorry. I . . ."

"Excuse us." The Ray Genet figure spoke again with an accent that sent chills—happy chills—up Sarah. "But I'm the only one who speaks English, so I will try to translate." The others smiled, handsome with their tanned faces and white teeth. Ooh, la la, thought Sarah, what hunks.

"My name is Jacques. You seem very young to be climbing, and so pretty."

Sarah blushed. "I'm seventeen and my name is Sarah."

All the men went "Ah . . . Sarah," with the accent on the second syllable.

"You are so healthy and strong. Going to *le* summit

or *le* descent?" Sarah was having a hard time concentrating on the meaning of his words because of his delightful accent.

"Summit. I wish it were down." She laughed. The men all shook their heads no.

"The summit is out of this world," Jacques said, kissing his right fingers with a big motion and opening up his hand.

"You've already been there? Congratulations."

The Frenchmen all started talking at once. "We made it to the summit. Every single one of us. But they want you to know that they want to go back up to the summit with you because it was so *magnifique.*"

Sarah smiled. "Wow. I wish you *could* come with me and give me courage." Jacques translated and they all beamed. Sarah shook their hands and they hugged her. Then everybody started talking all at once again, and Jacques tried to translate, but it got too confusing.

Soon they were all trying to communicate in pantomime, one guy huffing and puffing, another waving the French flag on the summit. The Frenchmen's enthusiasm was so contagious that they made Sarah believe she would make the summit. The knot in her stomach from Bobby's accident started melting away, until Jacques asked about it.

Sarah tried to explain, but the words wouldn't come out. So, instead, she shook her head and waved goodbye quickly. "Courage, Sarah," Jacques said, shaking her hand one more time. "You will make it. No one as young as you would be here if she did not have courage."

When they gathered for lunch, Sarah told Laura, Wendy, and Gabe about the Frenchmen. Sarah looked around. "Hey, where's Sam?"

123

Laura spoke quietly. "Sam's feeling light-headed and tired, so he's resting."

"But that doesn't sound like Sam," Sarah said. "Is he all right? And is Bobby any better?"

"Sam's fine," said Wendy. "Just needs a little rest like all of us. Bobby seems about the same."

"Sam's not overreacting to Bobby's accident, is he? I sure was for a while. Can Bobby keep climbing?"

Laura reached out and touched Sarah's arm. "Sarah, take it easy. They're doing fine. I'm going to see if they'll eat a little food."

Afterward, putting the lunch food away, Sarah noticed her new friends were dismantling their tents and packing up. She would miss these Frenchmen. They didn't expect anything of her, and in just a few minutes they had made her feel confident and strong.

In twelve days Sarah already had a history with her climbing mates. They'd seen her do some stupid things, and she'd seen them do the same. She needed a break—she was tired of always being watched. An only child, she was used to being alone, and yet the constant companionship always offered something interesting, if not enjoyable.

As she hung out her and her dad's gear in the sunshine after lunch, Sarah thought about a snow bath, but changed her mind. It wasn't *that* warm.

Gabe walked over with his camera. "Here. Why don't you spend the afternoon shooting pictures? Take your kind of photos and then keep the roll of film." How she had forgotten her camera, she'd never know. She'd made so many lists. Her dad was taking enough pictures for both of them, but Gabe was right—they weren't always her kind of photos.

"Thank you. But don't you want to use it today? It's so beautiful with the sun shining and the mountains below in the clouds. And look at those big boulders of rock above us."

"No, go ahead. I think we all need to do something different today."

Walking around shooting pictures, stripped down to her shorts and T-shirt and lathered with sun guard, Sarah hadn't felt this warm and relaxed since base camp. Later she sat in the sun and thought about how wonderful it was not to be worrying about a weather change every five minutes. Whiteouts and Bobby's accident seemed a million miles away. She'd reached 14. Maybe that would be enough. No, it wasn't enough, and thankfully she hadn't yet experienced any of the effects of altitude sickness.

Then she remembered Sam. He still hadn't gotten up. She wanted to go see him, but he was sharing a tent with Bobby. Just when she'd almost gotten up her nerve to stop by their tent, Gabe walked over.

"Thanks, Gabe, I had a great time shooting pictures. How do you say 'thank you' in Yup'ik?"

"*Quyana.*"

"*Quyana,*" Sarah tried, and they both laughed.

"You said earlier you didn't fit in at Mayruvik," Gabe said. "I've been thinking about that, and I think I understand. Maybe you helped them see things in a different way, not their way, but your way."

"I don't know. I just never knew how hard it could be to live in a different culture. But then sometimes I just loved the freedom of Mayurvik; being outdoors, spending time on the river and in the hills was so special to me."

"I miss the coast too." Gabe looked down the mountain for a while, then pulled something out of his pocket. He opened a plastic baggie and handed a piece to Sarah. "Here. Try some of this."

"What is it?" Sarah asked, taking a bite.

"Dried fish. Didn't you have any in Mayurvik?"

Sarah shook her head. "Mom and Mike did, but I never wanted to try it." Gabe stared at her. "I know. I was stupid and crazy. I wouldn't try anything. I was determined not to like anything, so my mom would feel guilty." Gabe and Sarah chewed silently for a while. "This is delicious."

Gabe nodded again. "I know. It's what keeps me going. You know, Sarah, I'm in a different culture here—mountain climbing."

"We all are."

"Maybe. But I've heard you talk of conquering the mountain. I believe in working with it."

"I do too. I've learned. Now I don't feel like I'm trying to beat the mountain. If it lets me climb the summit successfully, then both the mountain and I have won."

"You have changed, Sarah." Gabe looked around for a while, then continued talking. "You know, I have my feet in two cultures every day. It's so confusing and demanding. I had hoped climbing Denali might help me work out the confusion."

"Has it?"

"Some. But I don't know if I can ever really figure it out."

Gabe left and Sarah dozed in the sunshine until dinner, dreaming about taking a snow bath and then suddenly finding herself living in two cultures, her body torn apart in the middle. She felt a movement on her chin and opened her eyes with a squeal. Her dad was bending over her, tickling her chin with a feather. "Hey, sleepyhead. Time for dinner."

"I wasn't sleeping, I just . . ." Then Sarah stopped herself and smiled. She had a right to be tired. She'd just climbed to 14,000 feet above altitude, something most people would never dream of doing.

Her dad looked so happy. "How was your day, Dad? You weren't even gone long enough to get me worried."

"A piece of cake," he said, rubbing his hands together.

"Even the part near Bobby's crevasse?"

"Oh, so it's Bobby's crevasse now. I'm sure he'd happily give it back. Sarah, I'm glad you rested today."

"Dad, I could have—"

"Hold on. Of course, you could have. I'm just glad you took it easy. Would you stop being so defensive all the time?"

After dinner Sarah stayed up late drinking tea and talking to Wendy and Laura. They sat admiring the way the midnight sun illuminated the basin and the mountains with colors of orange and pink, deepening to purple and red as the evening wore on.

"Doesn't this remind you in a way of the winter northern lights? Nature celebrating the seasons with color," Laura said, stretching out her long, beautiful legs. "I guess that's what keeps me in Alaska, these moments that capture you and stay in your heart all year long."

Wendy nodded, and Sarah wondered why she didn't feel the same way. She wished she could.

The next morning, Day 13, people rolled out of their tents for a late breakfast. Then Doug and Tim set up a fixed line for practice, in preparation for tomorrow, weather permitting. The climb between 15,000 and 16,000 feet included the fixed-line section, the toughest section of the whole trip.

Before they practiced, Doug explained how it

127

worked. "Gang, this section of climbing is a solid piece of ice, so be prepared. The fixed line was already set up at the beginning of the climbing season. So all we have to do is get clipped into it when we get there. Like this." Doug demonstrated how to set up the jumar on the line and clip it to the chest harness. "We'll still be roped in as always. The fixed line is an emergency measure, in case you fall. Don't ever use the rope to pull you up. Anyway, it's close to the ground, so I don't think that would be too much fun." Everybody laughed.

This was fun, Sarah thought, when it wasn't the real thing. It reminded her of being back in Talkeetna and practicing the crevasse rescue, so long ago when they didn't know one another and had no idea they'd really end up rescuing somebody.

Bobby wasn't at breakfast, though he did come out for the fixed-line practice. He went back to his tent right afterward, so Sarah still didn't get a chance to talk to him. She had put it off for two days, and she hated it when she procrastinated about something she knew she should do. How hard could it be to tell him how brave he was and how glad she was that he was all right? But was he all right?

He seemed so different since the accident. Instead of joking and mouthing off during the fixed-line practice, he hardly said a word. In a strange sort of way Sarah missed the old cocky Bobby. This pale version was someone she didn't know. At least before, it had been simple just to dislike the old Bobby.

At lunch Sarah sat with Sam, glad to see he was his old self again. Wendy started talking about the fixed-line section and how it wasn't going to be a problem.

"Right, Wendy. Confidence. That's what we all need," said Sarah's dad.

Sometimes Sarah wished Wendy weren't always so

cheerful. Was her dad interested in Wendy? He had told her once, when he started dating again after the divorce, that he didn't like women who came on too strong. But what about men who came on too strong?

It would never work between them, Sarah thought, as she looked over at Wendy. Wendy was strong, but she was also nice, almost too accommodating. Her dad needed somebody who would give it right back to him. But her mother was strong. What good did that do?

Gabe started to speak and everyone quieted down. "I don't know . . . sometimes being too confident can get you in trouble. Being careful and aware, that's what I've learned is important in hunting and in climbing."

Sarah went back to the tent and tried to write a letter to her mother, but all she could think about was Gabe's advice to be careful and aware. She had planned to write to her mother often, in Fairbanks, where she and Mike were taking summer courses. She was going to send letters out with parties descending the mountain because she knew that her mother and Mike would be worried. But Sarah couldn't find the words to express the exhilaration and the struggles she was experiencing. Her moods changed so quickly, and she didn't want her mother to misunderstand and worry after she got a letter.

So, instead, she picked up *Wuthering Heights*. Talk about struggles. Catherine and Heathcliff, little Cathy, Hareton, and the rest. They knew how to cause problems for themselves and each other. Sarah laughed. That almost made her feel normal.

chapter

THE nights were the worst. Sarah would be all right during the daytime, but at night, when the sky darkened slightly, and Sarah could hear her dad's or Sam's snoring, the dreams would come.

Sarah didn't get up for breakfast the next morning. She could hear them all moving around, but when she looked outside the tent and saw the poor visibility—and remembered last night's radio forecast from base camp—she knew they wouldn't be climbing today. She was munching on a breakfast bar and listening to the radio on the earphones when her dad came into the tent.

He tapped her on the shoulder. "Hi, aren't you coming to breakfast?"

Lifting up her earphones, she said, "No. Why? We're not going anywhere."

"Well, excuse me for bothering you, but it's cold. I need another layer."

"See? Why should I come out?"

"You know, you're being a brat, and I hate it when you lose your confidence. I want you to make it so badly."

"I haven't lost my confidence. I'm just nervous about the fixed line. Can't a person express their feelings? You worry about yourself. I have to take care of me."

Sarah wanted to stay in the tent all day, but Tim made her take a walk after lunch. "If you don't get a little exercise, you'll be a weakling tomorrow. You've got to practice working out at this altitude."

"Tim, I'm so tired."

"Of course, you're tired. Just living at this high altitude is hard work. But you've got to put up with it if you want the summit badly enough."

Sarah tried to change the subject. "How are Sam and Bobby?"

"They're hanging in there, but both could probably use a visit."

Sarah went by their tent, figuring she could handle talking to Bobby in front of Sam. But both were asleep, or at least their eyes were closed. So she went right back to her tent and pulled out her journal. One of her mom's quotes might cheer her up.

> *"We are the flow, we are the ebb,*
> *We are the weavers, we are the web."*
>
> —Shekinah Mountainwater

DAY 14—two weeks into the trip.

What is this supposed to mean? What web am I making? A strong one to support me up the mountain or a prison to hold

131

me in? Flow and ebb, rivers, the ocean, life.
I know I have to flow more. I'm even more
uptight than Dad now. I have to slow down
in my head. My body's slowed down enough.

Her dad checked on her before dinner. "Please come out." She knew he meant well, but she felt like a captive of the mountain and the weather, unable to get free from Denali's web.

The next morning, Day 15, the sun was shining brightly and Sarah woke up happy and rested. For the first time since Bobby's accident, she hadn't dreamed about it. She was the first one up, including the guides. This was a big day. They would push on to 16,200 feet, maybe even 17,000 feet.

All through breakfast, Sarah concentrated on being positive, thinking about how she would sail through the fixed-line section with ease—until Bobby shared his news.

"This is it, gang. I'm throwing the towel in." He tried to sound like the old Bobby, but it didn't play.

"Bobby, you can't. We gotta do this together," Sarah said, not believing her mouth had uttered the words. She sounded like Wendy.

"Sarah, were you the one throwing up all night? Are you dehydrated and weak in the arms? I just can't do it anymore."

Tim said, "Hey, Bobby. Take it easy." Then he turned to the others. "Doug, Gabe, and I agree with Bobby that he just hasn't recovered fully enough from the fall to have the stamina to climb right now. So he's going to wait it out here today and see how he feels tonight."

Sarah went over and sat next to Bobby. "I'm sorry. What I meant to say is that it won't be the same without you."

"Right. You won't have me getting in your way anymore, driving you nuts." This sounded more like the old Bobby. Sarah and Bobby sat talking, as the others packed up around them. "We'll miss you. I'll miss you."

"Is this the real Sarah Janson talking? The girl who can't stand my guts?" Bobby looked down and started jabbing his boot into the snow. "You helped save my life, but you still have your 'Don't come near me' sign up, so I've never even said thank you."

Bobby stopped and looked up at Sarah. "I'm sorry. I wouldn't be here without your quick thinking. Thank you. But you're so confusing. Now when I'm about to leave, you act like we're friends."

His feelings are so strong, thought Sarah, but his voice so weak. "Maybe . . . Maybe we could be. Maybe I did judge you too soon."

"You bet you did. But now it's too late. You're all going to the summit without me." Then Bobby stopped himself. "But at least I'm alive."

"I'm really sorry it had to turn out this way, Bobby. I've never seen anyone braver than you that day. I would have fallen apart."

"No, you wouldn't. But thanks, I needed to hear that." Bobby turned to look at the mountain, taking Sarah's hand in his. "I guess you'll just have to make that summit for both of us."

"You might be better by tomorrow."

"Maybe." But he didn't sound too sure. Bobby

dropped Sarah's hand and stood up. "Oh, by the way. You're all right. All you need to do is chill out a little."

For the first time, Sarah laughed at one of Bobby's comments, relieved that some of the old cockiness was still there. But she felt sad at the same time. Bobby couldn't hide his great disappointment. She still didn't really like him, but she cared about him. He was part of their team. And now that he was showing a new side, the climb might be over for him.

Tim would stay with Bobby at 14, working out with him and keeping him company. Then both of them could head up to 17 with the others tomorrow.

Sarah would pray all day for that to happen. Up here on this mountain she had become closer to God and the spirit world, and believed that they were watching over them as they climbed.

Sarah would miss Tim. She had come so much to depend on his friendship and support. She appreciated how slow he was to judge and how quick to praise.

Tim and Bobby waved them off. When Sarah looked back one more time, Bobby was gone and Tim was just a figure in the basin, lost among all the tents.

Tim was right. Climbing was different after 14. Suddenly they seemed to move so much slower. The cold, dry, thin air made it hard for Sarah to breathe, and she felt weak. It was as if the *oomph* had been taken out of her body. Part of that, Sarah knew, was because she had to wear all the equipment and supplies on her back. The sleds had gotten lighter and lighter up the mountain as they ate the food. Now that they had left the sleds behind, Sarah's back felt the burden.

Progress seemed sluggish all along the line. At least she wasn't the only one having trouble, Sarah thought, as she shivered and pulled down the flaps on her cap. If she were injured instead of Bobby, she could be in a warm sleeping bag right now, and this huge weight would be off her back. Bobby should be here. For all his bravado, Bobby needed to prove something too. And he had dreamed of climbing Denali for years. This was a new dream for her, and here she was, complaining all the way to the top.

Climbing up the thousand-foot upgrade out of the camp, they hit a huge snowdrift left by a recent avalanche, and began crawling through waist-deep snow. After a few feet, Doug stopped. So even he got tired, Sarah thought. Sarah pulled out her water bottle from her pack. She was so thirsty and tired. She knew she hadn't drunk enough fluids the last three days. It was so hard to remember when she wasn't climbing. But now she couldn't get enough to drink.

Sooner than expected, they were out of the snowdrift and back to snow-covered ice. Sarah jammed her ice ax in the snow, grateful that this rough section was over—for now. She began to find her rhythm again as her pants dried out in the wind, and she was no longer cold.

Why did things always have to go wrong? Tim loved climbing, and Bobby wanted to make the summit so badly, yet they weren't going to make it. Maybe you shouldn't want things too badly.

Her dad wanted a divorce, and her mom didn't. Yet now her mom was happy with Mike, and her dad was lonely.

Finally, they reached 15,000 feet and the fixed-line section, where they would climb the actual buttress. The refreshment break of juice and gorp tasted great, especially since Sarah had hardly eaten any breakfast this morning because of Bobby's news.

Before they started up the line, Doug reviewed the procedure. "Okay, gang, attach your extra piece of rope to your carabiner and clip it to your waist harness. Everybody got that?'' Doug checked around the group. ''Now attach that rope to your jumar ascender. When you come to the start of the fixed line, attach the jumar to the fixed line, and you are ready to go.'' Doug and Gabe walked around, looking at everyone's setup.

''Remember, this is just a safety precaution in case you fall. Crawl up this slope if you have to, but no matter what, keep on going. It is so long and slippery, one thousand feet, that you don't want to stop and slow anybody else down. Just keep climbing and don't use the fixed line to pull yourself up. It's lying on the snow, just to stop you if you fall. Don't worry. The jumar ascender can only move up, not down. So it will definitely grab the rope if you hit the ground.''

Sarah reviewed the steps in her head as she lined up behind Doug. But looking up the long slope, she stopped short. What if she slipped and fouled up the whole line? No, stop it, she thought. She was going to be positive all the way. She had to think positively or she would never make it.

Moving carefully, Sarah let her crampons grip the snow. Being clipped into the fixed line did give her an added sense of security, along with knowing they were still roped into one another on the line. Planting her ice ax, Sarah began slowly, ever so slowly, moving up the slippery ice and crawling along with her fellow June Bugs.

She stared straight ahead, afraid to look to the side or behind her. One bad fall and a climber could go cartwheeling down the mountain, pulling the rest of the rope team with her. They would all slide down as if on sleds, their flesh rubbing against the snow, snow pouring down their necks, carrying them to a death of suffocation in the snow. Sarah stifled a scream in her throat.

Starting to hyperventilate, she closed her mouth and focused on her breathing. No, that was crazy, she told herself. That was what the fixed line was for, to catch you if you fell. One hand in front of the other. I can do this. I have to stay positive. I will stay positive.

Clearing her mind of all negative thoughts and focusing solely on moving her body forward, Sarah finally hit a routine. The farther up she climbed, the safer she felt. Breathing hard, she kept repeating one foot, one foot, one hand, one hand, as she crawled up the steep slope.

Joyfully, Sarah looked up to see the drudge march was over. Sixteen appeared at the top, a wide, open spot with a majestic view of the huge, snowy tundra on all sides and the glacier below. She had made it through the roughest section of the trip, and now she could relax and enjoy this snowy desert. After unroping and stretching her cramped legs, Sarah hugged her dad and, surprised, he hugged her back. Her body was so tired from tensing her muscles for so long, but her heart was happy. She hadn't stopped. She hadn't let the others down. She had kept on going, not with muscle, but with finesse, as Tim would say.

Sarah would think about climbing back down for the rest of their gear later. Right now, she was going to pretend she was at Mount Bachelor, sunning at lunch, after a busy morning of downhill skiing.

Skiing. She could just imagine meeting Bobby on the ski slopes. He with his perfectly matched outfit and smooth moves. They would have hated each other instantly.

Sarah looked over at Sam. He seemed to move as if drunk, pulling a candy bar out of his bag and then awkwardly sitting down on his pack. It was a strain to breathe, and Sarah didn't want to waste her energy talking too much, but she felt so worried about Sam that she got up and went over to him.

"You doing all right?"

Sam nodded, breathing hard. "I'm okay. Just a little tired."

"Me too. That section was tough, wasn't it?" Sam nodded again, his eyes closed. Sarah put her arm around Sam's shoulder, trying to cheer him up. "Sam, I miss your singing. Guess we'll have to wait awhile for that." Sam didn't answer, just kept his eyes closed.

After the break, Doug put them to work digging a cache for their extra supplies. Sarah tried not to take Sam's reaction personally. But if he wasn't mad at her, he must be sick. Was it altitude sickness? Is this how it started?

The shallow wind in the bowl had hardened the snow and made it difficult to dig. "Sarah, that hole isn't deep enough," Doug said. She knew it wasn't deep enough, but she couldn't push her shovel any harder.

"Keep digging. Remember what I said about those ravens. We might be in desperate need of this food later, and they could have beaten us to it. Come on, everybody. Let's work a little harder. I want to get back to 14."

Sarah gritted her teeth and tried to put more arm muscle into her digging. But her body was tired. Didn't Doug think she wanted to get back to camp too? He could be so bossy sometimes, as though they were a bunch of school kids or something. She missed Tim. He always treated people with dignity. Thank God Gabe was around.

Later Sarah actually enjoyed the quick descent on the fixed line, even though it was icy. This time around she had more confidence and focused on appreciating the excitement instead of the danger. At both breaks she kept her eye on Sam from afar. Selfishly, she wanted her energetic friend back.

Right before the avalanche section, the weather turned cold. Sarah's body was starting to react against these temperature swings. It had been hot at 16, especially after sweating through the fixed-line section and digging the cache, and yet now she was freezing as they crawled through snow.

At dinner Sam still wasn't talking, though Sarah sat quietly nearby. She felt that she was losing another friend, and not even Bobby was around to bug her. Bobby didn't come out for dinner although Laura went in to talk to him. Instead, Laura and Sarah's dad ate dinner in the tent with him.

Sarah offered to be on KP duty to distract herself and was grateful when Laura offered too.

"How're you doing?" Laura said as she put away the food. "You seem a little down."

"Aren't you?"

"No, I'm thrilled. I can't believe we made it to 16 without too much trouble. Sixteen—that's a milestone, fixed line and all."

"But Laura, everything's changed." Sarah could hear the whine in her voice and knew how her dad would hate it. "It looks like Bobby and Tim won't be going on with us. Sam acts sick and crabby and won't talk to me. And I don't know if this trip is bringing my dad and me any closer."

"Slow down. One thing at a time. Yes, I feel very badly about Bobby and Tim. But if I let it get to me, I'll never make the summit. And that's not going to do anybody any good, if we just give up. Sam will reach out when he needs you. He's fighting off altitude sickness and that's pretty serious."

"Does he have altitude sickness for sure?"

"Doug seems to think so. He's treating him with aspirin and thinks Sam can lick it, if he has enough time to adjust to the altitude."

"How come nobody told me?"

"What's there to say? We all knew he wasn't doing well and . . ."

"And what? I couldn't handle it, just like I couldn't handle Bobby's accident?"

"Hey, don't get mad at me. What are you talking about? You handled Bobby's accident like a pro. I'm still bothered by it, too, but I can't dwell on it."

"Really?"

"Really. You can't either. Instead, concentrate on making the summit. Everything else will take care of itself. Even with your dad."

Sarah breathed deep into her chest, slowly releasing the air and trying to relax her body. Then she looked at her friend. "Good night. Thanks for listening."

Laura gave Sarah a hug. "Good night, Sarah. Sweet dreams."

chapter 15

DAY 16 dawned overcast and snowy as they departed. It would be another long day, but Doug seemed to think they were up to it. "We're over the hump, guys. You all are adjusting to the altitude change well, and your energy is strong. Let's keep it up."

Even though Tim and Bobby would not be with them, Sarah did feel better, especially when she looked over at Sam, who also seemed to have more energy. Maybe they were over the hump, but not the mountain, she thought, and laughed.

The snowy avalanche area of yesterday became today's easy journey. The wind had blown the snow completely away. Sarah tried to smile at this luck, but the weather was becoming more and more unpredictable, and her stomach had begun to register every change.

She had developed gastritis last year, and her mother kept worrying that this trip might set it off again. Pre-ulcer, the doctor had called it. Surprisingly, Sarah hadn't even noticed her stomach on this trip, except on the plane ride and last night, when it kept hurting and hurting as she tried to go to sleep. Tim had said the mountain uncovers hidden weaknesses.

Today when they reached the fixed-line section, Wendy had trouble getting hooked in. She was right behind Gabe on the lead team.

"Wendy, what are you doing? Let's get the show on the road."

"I can't get this dumb—" Then she turned on Doug. "Would you just shut up? I'm sick and tired of hearing you yell at people. How about treating us with a little respect?"

Doug was silent for a moment and then gave Wendy his teasing, boyish smile. "Sorry, ma'am. Just didn't want to freeze out the rest of the folks." Then he swept his hat off and bowed toward her. "Take your time."

"Oh, you big bouf," Wendy said. "You may not believe it, but most people find me a competent individual with a good self-image. And I plan to stay that way, summit or not." But all the while that she said this Doug kept smiling at her, and Wendy couldn't help laughing.

Gabe helped Wendy get her carabiner fixed and the group took off up the fixed line, another crisis averted. Sarah wasn't scared today, but she felt a nagging deep inside that she couldn't get rid of. She had been ready to yell at Doug herself when Wendy started laughing. If she couldn't keep her own frustrations contained, how did she expect others to? She wanted everyone else to be in a good mood, but was she that much fun to be around?

Snowflakes began to fall and fall and fall. The wind started blowing, fog set in, and soon the visibility was near zero. Sarah groaned inside when she realized the

142

work ahead of them—building snow walls, four or five feet high around their tents in weather like this would be imperative. Doug didn't want to stop at the campsite at 16,200 feet because it wasn't as safe as the one at 16,300 feet, but the weather was so bad, they had no choice.

Her hands freezing, Sarah kept sawing the snow, hoping this would warm them up. Although her down gloves kept her fingers warm, they were so bulky she could hardly move the saw, so she had to wear her lighter-weight gloves to complete the task.

Sarah didn't think she could last much longer. She looked over at her dad, and his face was all scrunched up in pain too. Sam's tent stood whipping in the wind. He was inside battling full-blown altitude sickness. He'd been slurring his words all day and hadn't been able to keep anything down.

Sarah knew that if he didn't eat something soon, he'd be too weak to keep climbing. Doug and Gabe had settled Sam in their tent as soon as they had arrived, hoping the extra rest would make a difference.

Day 17. The constant whooshing wind had stopped. Sarah woke out of a deep sleep. All was quiet. The storm had passed.

Doug called into their tent. "It's still the middle of the night, folks, and cold like the dickens, but it's clear. So we're going to head on up to 17 with our last set of supplies. It's better camping up there, anyway, and hanging out there will help us adjust to the altitude better."

"But how's Sam?" Sarah called out as she got dressed. She and her dad were alone in the tent.

"He's holding on. I gave him the drug Diamox before he went to bed. I've seen it do wonders in some cases. And this morning he does seem a little better. Says he's strong enough to head up.''

"Terrific," said Sarah's dad. "We kinda miss him in the tent."

But as Sarah grabbed something to eat before they took off, she noticed Sam was just standing there. "Come on, Sam. You've gotta eat to keep up your strength."

"I can't keep it down, so just leave . . . me . . . alone." His voice was weak.

"I'm sorry, Sam. I just want to make the summit with you." Sam shook his head and turned away. Sarah went back to her dried meat, and felt the tears well up in her eyes. Had she said the wrong thing again?

Loading up her backpack, Sarah saw Sam eating and talking to Wendy. Okay. She didn't care how he treated her as long as he got better. She strained to make out the conversation in the wind.

"Throbbing headache, diarrhea, tired all the time . . . I can't seem to get motivated. I should have quit smoking . . . years ago. Now it's catching up with me . . . I was a fool to think I could climb . . . this mountain."

"Shush, Sam." Wendy put her arm around Sam's shoulder. "Don't say any more. Is the Diamox helping?"

"I don't know." And then he shook his head.

"Sam, you can do it. I know you can. Just drink some fluids and walk around. You'll feel better soon." Sam smiled feebly as Wendy went over to pack up her tent.

Packing just enough supplies for a couple of days at 17 and a summit bid, the six other climbers worked quickly while Sam rested. They were running a race against time—any minute Sarah felt that the weather might change.

When they started off, Sam was roped in between Doug and Sarah. At least she could keep an eye on him today.

It was snowing heavily at the Crow's Nest, the camp at 17,000 feet, when they arrived two hours later. But at least Sam was still climbing. Sarah's own breathing was becoming much more labored, and she couldn't believe how much longer it took just to do simple things like take off her pack. The winds had picked up again during their climb. Several other parties looked as if they'd been settled in for a while—not a good sign.

The thought of building snow walls again tonight made Sarah want to drop in exhaustion before they even started. But her first concern was Sam. Immediately after they checked for crevasses and unroped, both she and Doug went over to him. He was breathing hard and was so weak and disoriented he could hardly stand on his feet.

"He's got hypothermia, Doug. All we need to do is get him warmed up."

"No, Sarah, this isn't hypothermia. He's not shivering. Looks like his altitude sickness has gotten worse. He needs fluids, carbohydrates, and rest." Doug turned to Gabe and said, "You and John put up a tent, and I'll get him into dry clothes and a sleeping bag. Sarah and Laura, heat up some stew and hot cider."

Fixing the stew, Sarah kept berating herself. I shouldn't have pushed him this morning. He could die on this mountain, and it'll be my fault. All because I wouldn't leave him alone and let him make his own decision.

Later Doug was subdued and serious. "If he doesn't get markedly better in a couple of hours, he'll have to

145

head back down. We've got no choice. If we wait until he's in critical condition, we're playing with fate. In the end, only Sam knows what his body can take."

Sarah tried not to cry, telling herself that she had to be strong for the journey ahead. But she hated the thought of losing another team member, especially Sam, her friend from the beginning.

Sam got worse. An hour later Doug sent word that Sarah should bring some more stew to the tent. She tried to feed Sam, but he kept his mouth closed, his breathing getting shallower and shallower. Then he started mumbling and clawing at the tent walls. "I can't breathe. Let me out of here. I can't breathe." Frantic about what to do, Sarah looked around for Doug, but he was gone.

She took Sam in her arms. "We'll get you out of here in a minute, Sam. Take it easy." Softly, she started singing him a lullaby until Doug and Gabe finally returned.

"I'm sorry we took so long. I was trying to radio down to 14 and set up an emergency plan. He's got to descend to a lower altitude immediately. There's no other choice. If he leaves now, he can go on his own two feet. That's much safer than trying to take him down in an emergency bivouac sack later."

While Gabe and her dad got Sam ready to travel, Doug spoke to Sarah, Laura, and Wendy outside. "Don't worry. Sam will be fine as soon as we get him back to 14, where there's the medical tent. Usually a change of altitude is all that is needed to snap a person out of this. And if that doesn't work, another Summit guide, maybe even Tim, will take him all the way to base camp and fly him out, if necessary. He's going to be all right."

Doug stared right at Sarah. "I hate leaving you guys,

but you'll be fine, as long as you stay put. I thought about having Gabe come with us or asking one of you to volunteer to come down to 14, but you all need every minute you can get up here, adjusting to the altitude, if you want to make 20,320 feet.'' Doug paused to rest. ''See what I mean? This is taking a lot out of me, just talking.'' He looked at the three women and Sarah's dad, who had now joined them. ''Another expedition is leaving right now for 14, so Sam and I will join them. I haven't said it enough. You're all very tough, and I'm very proud of you.''

Sarah knew Sam had to go, but it was so hard. ''Doug, all Sam has dreamed of is making the summit. Isn't there anything else that can be done for him?''

''No, Sarah.''

Sam came up, breathing hard, his face white. ''Doug is right. My body just won't . . . take me . . . any farther. Like Tim said, I've made the summit . . . in myself. You do the rest for both of us.'' Sarah held back the tears as she hugged her friend good-bye.

Watching Sam slowly creep down the mountain, Sarah couldn't believe this was the same Sam who had spent the early days of the trip laughing and singing. Once after cracking a joke, he had quoted her one of his favorite sayings. ''Sarah, always remember what Sarah Bernhardt once said: 'Life begets life. Energy creates energy. It is by spending oneself that one becomes rich.' ''

SARAH slept the rest of the day after Sam left. The howling wind and the flapping of the tent wove in and out of her dreams. She tried to sit up, but she was so weak that she lay back down. She rolled over and moved her hand around, looking for her journal. She opened it and began to read.

I am going to die on this mountain. The mountain is out to get me. Just like Ray Genet and Pete Huddleston and maybe even Sam, I am going to die. But I'll never leave. I'll stay on the mountain to haunt other climbers and laugh at them for thinking they could conquer me. For I am one with Denali now. I am Denali.

I don't want to die. I want to see my mother again. I want to go running and eat ice cream and fall in love.

Sarah started crying. She couldn't remember writing this journal. What had happened? Then she remembered. Sam was gone. Sam had gone down the mountain with Doug.

She tried to stop her tears, but they just kept coming and coming. Then when she heard her dad outside the tent, she buried her head down into her sleeping bag.

"Sarah, are you awake? I thought I heard you moaning. Sarah?" Her father came into the tent and gently began shaking her. "Sarah, are you all right?"

"No, my head hurts. Just let me rest."

"Sarah, come on. Laura and Gabe are fixing up some dinner. Why don't you join us? It's nice enough that we can even eat outside." Sarah shook her head. "Please. It will make you feel better."

"Just leave me alone."

"Sarah, you need to get out of this tent. You haven't left it since late this morning. Waiting it out in these small tents in weather from hell is driving us all batty."

"Not you. Nothing seems to get to you." Sarah was crying openly now. "I told Sam to eat and look what happened to him. For all we know he's dead right now. Nobody accused him of faking." Sarah rolled over and closed her eyes. Finally, she heard her father leave.

Sarah tried to sleep some more but couldn't. The walls of the domed yellow tent started closing in on her, like big weights pressing on her chest. The sleeping bag was suffocating her. Ripping it off, she sat up. She couldn't breathe. She had to get fresh air. But she was tired, so tired.

Sarah moved over to the door and tried to unzip it. She had to get out of here. She would go down the mountain, free at last. Free and warm and well fed.

But then her dad was back in the tent with Gabe, kneeling beside her. "Sarah, what are you doing? You're out of your sleeping bag and not even dressed. You could freeze to death."

He pulled Sarah back into her bag and then handed her clothes to her.

"I don't want these," she said, shoving them back. "God away. Can't you see I'm sick?" Sarah jerked her head around quickly, darting her eyes back and forth. "Where are Laura and Wendy? Has something happened to them too?"

Gabe and her dad exchanged looks, and then her dad spoke. "Wendy's in the tent with Laura. Laura's having a bit of a rough time right now, but it's not serious."

Sarah sat up and grabbed her dad's arm. "See? See? Everybody's sick. Sam, me, Laura."

Gabe spoke for the first time. "Sarah, you're going to get through this. I don't think you have altitude sickness. You're not slurring your speech and your body is still strong. You can relax for a couple of days." Gabe looked at Sarah for a moment and took a breath. "You know, sometimes people think they have altitude sickness, but the symptoms clear up. Come out and eat something, then come over to my tent and play some poker with your dad and me."

Sarah looked at his dark, calm face. Then she felt her head. It was dizzy and feverish. "Poker? You don't play poker. Has everybody gone crazy?" Her voice sounded far away, as though she were talking underwater. "And what do you know? You've never climbed Denali before."

"Well, I guess I'm just a fast learner." Gabe

laughed, and then Sarah's dad laughed, and then Sarah started laughing, an out-of-control hysterical laugh that suddenly turned into sobs. She started to shiver and let her dad put the down coat around her shoulders.

"Sarah, we need you. We can't afford to lose any more of our team. Our Yup'ik elders teach us we will come back to life later as a newborn after we die. Bobby and Sam will climb Denali someday, maybe as themselves or maybe as one of their descendants named Bobby or Sam, who will climb Denali twenty or a hundred years from now." Gabe took Sarah by the shoulders. "But you, I see you climbing Denali now."

Sarah stopped crying and looked up at Gabe.

"Sarah, I knew the minute I saw you that you were strong and determined. No seventeen-year-old girl who isn't very strong and very brave would attempt such a feat. You had to have had a very special calling for you to be here. Don't go deaf now. Bobby has learned that he can be weak and still be strong. Sam has learned that he can push himself only so far and still be complete. *You* must learn to let your mind help your body go as far as it can." Gabe stopped and looked down at the floor.

"Gabe, what have you learned?" Sarah's voice sounded strong to her ears.

Gabe closed his eyes and the tent was quiet with only the wind blowing outside. "I am still trying to learn how to serve my people and at the same time serve myself."

"And Gabe, what do I still need to learn?" Sarah's father asked. Sarah had forgotten her dad was in the tent.

"That sometimes we come to know God, *ella yua,* through our children." Gabe nodded and left the tent.

But a few seconds later he called back, "And Sarah, remember, sometimes a father can be right."

Neither Sarah nor her dad spoke. She had so much to think about, and her head was pounding. Finally, her father spoke, so quietly, in such a begging voice, that Sarah thought it was someone else, "Honey, you've got to at least eat something, even if it's just for strength to descend the mountain."

"Dad, what do you know about giving up?" Her voice was again weak. "You've always done what you wanted to do, what your mind told your body to do."

"Sarah, damn it. Stop the poor pity me act. You've been burning up this mountain the whole trip. You've got more guts than any kid I know. Use 'em. You're too close to give up now."

Sarah lay back down and thought about all that had happened.

"I'll go now, Sarah. But first I have to follow through on a promise." Sarah thought she heard a catch in her dad's voice. "I don't know about fathers, Sarah, but I do know mothers can be right. I've been saving something for you—something your mother said to give you when you most needed it. I've debated all through the trip when to do this. That first day when I yelled at you about the sleeping pad and you were so mad you almost got back on the plane—should I have done it then? Or how about the night we had to build snow walls in a windchill of forty below, or the day after Bobby fell into the crevasse? But always in the end you got feisty or furious or found something deep within to bring you back and keep you going." Sarah's dad looked away. "But today you're different. You're not fighting anymore, and it scares me." He started tugging on the pull string of his down coat.

"When I first signed you up for this expedition, Tim

asked me to think about how you would feel if you had to give up at a certain point, how most seventeen-year-olds don't have the mind-set to focus on such a goal or the lung capacity to complete it.

"And I said, but Sarah's different. She's always been older than her years. She's so steady, and so physically strong. And she's a fighter. What a fighter. But she also knows when to stop, when her body can't take her any farther. She learned that last summer in the marathon."

Her dad grabbed Sarah and hugged her hard. "Sarah, Tim believed me, and you convinced him too."

"I never knew you had to convince them to take me," Sarah said, whispering into her dad's shoulder.

"I didn't want to lessen your confidence. You were so excited. For the first time all year you sounded happy when I talked to you over the phone. You can head back down, Sarah." Sarah's dad pulled away from her and stared into her eyes. "There's no shame in it. No seventeen-year-old girl has ever climbed higher. But you're so close." He gripped Sarah's shoulders hard.

"Dad, aren't you scared?"

"Sarah, I'm so damn scared for both of us I feel like I'm going to wet my pants half the time. But it's too cold." He laughed and then stopped. "Some days on this trip I have wondered why I have allowed, even encouraged, you to do this. But then all I have to do is look over and see you trudging up the mountain, never giving up, and I smile and keep going too. Here." Her dad thrust a letter into her hand. "I'll be in Gabe's tent whenever you need me."

Sarah held the light blue envelope in her hand and then smelled it. She could just picture her mother sitting at the kitchen table in Mayurvik, writing this letter and looking out on the tundra.

153

Dear Sarah,

You will probably wonder why I haven't said all this before. But it is only now as you sit in your bedroom sorting through your climbing gear, that I seem to be able to put my feelings into words. I'm so proud of you. So amazed that we have raised a daughter who wants to climb Mount McKinley before she's even out of high school. The very idea of climbing the tallest mountain in North America overwhelms me. But then you always have overwhelmed me too. So strong and independent. You haven't needed me very much, just like your father, and sometimes that's hard. But most of the time it's wonderful to think that I have a teenage daughter who will be able to find her own way in the world.

Though I can't fathom doing it, I really wish I were with you. Maybe sometime we can take an adventure together. For that I envy you and your father. I made a choice last summer when I married Mike and brought you to Alaska, a choice that directly affected your life. I have cried to see your unhappiness this past year in Mayurvik. Economic theory states that the true cost of anything is what we give up in order to have it. I gave up our life in Eugene, so that I could have a life with Mike. I have to take responsibility for that.

I have worried that you were climbing McKinley only to get away from me and Mike and Mayurvik. You have been so mixed up and troubled in spirit. I have tried to help, but that didn't seem to be what you needed or wanted. Yes, I do think you want to get away from Mayurvik, but I also have come to see that you desperately need to spend *time with your father and spend time testing your own strength.*

I close with this wonderful quote, which is what finally convinced me that I should give my approval to your expedition up McKinley. Not that I didn't fight it every inch of the way. I'm sorry for that. But only when you become a mother yourself will you realize just how much we worry. I love you, Sarah, and will pray for you every moment, until you are safely down the mountain. I know you will give it everything you've got to finish your incredible journey.

> *"Let her*
> *swim, climb mountain peaks, pilot airplanes,*
> *battle against the elements, take risks,*
> *go out for adventure, and*
>   *she will not*
> *feel before the world . . . timidity."*

—Simone de Beauvoir

Love,
Mother

Silent tears streamed down Sarah's face. How could she be so lucky?

Sarah reread the letter several times aloud, then put it inside her journal. Dressing slowly, she tried to stretch out her shoulders and neck. Emerging from the tent, she stood staring at the whipping orange flags and piles of climbing gear. I am part of this, she thought. I belong here. Denali is in me, not against me. Fighting against Denali is like fighting against myself.

The shadow—the weak, scared part of herself that

she never wanted to admit existed. Ms. Harris told Sarah she would have to integrate the shadow before she could succeed. Had she finally done that?

What would happen to her shadow if she gave up? She was scared and tired of working so hard, so very tired. But you can't give up now, her shadow said. You're too stubborn. You think you're better than most. Sarah, you can still breathe. You're not slurring your words or throwing up. You're not sick like Sam or injured like Bobby. Be stubborn like me, Sarah. Remember, your shadow is always with you. Sarah looked around. She could feel her shadow within her.

Later that night while the others slept, Sarah kept tossing and turning, reaching for her dad, then pushing him away. The wind was shrieking wildly, and Sarah woke up sweating. The noise of the fly sheets whipping against the tent split her brain, as if trying to let her shadow in or out, in or out. They could never make a summit bid in this kind of weather and Doug would never get back to them safely. She'd be stuck here with her shadow for days and weeks, maybe years. She had to go to the bathroom, but she pushed it out of her mind. She couldn't go out in this wind.

Sarah started panting. She couldn't last another moment up here. Beside her, she heard her dad whisper, "Take slow, deep breaths. Take slow, deep breaths." Her dad kept repeating it until Sarah felt her eyes close.

Sarah dreamed of a man standing at her mother's side during labor, repeating, "Take slow, deep breaths." Then a baby came out. The man was so happy, kissing the baby's face and caressing the baby's hands. How he must love this baby. She tried and tried, but all was fuzzy. She couldn't make out the face of the man or the baby, either.

chapter 17

DAY 18.

I am the quiet after the storm. Like the monarch butterfly, I have protected myself, keeping my dark side to the outside, my bright side turned in. It is time to turn that bright side out. To show that to others. It's time to be Artemis again and finish this journey.

OUTSIDE, the weather had cleared, but their final camp, three thousand feet from the summit, was now covered in six feet of snow. Yet Sarah could still see all the way up and down the mountain. Below her, the two sides of the saucer-shaped area dropped three thousand feet. That must be why they called it the Crow's Nest, she thought.

Sarah looked up at the sun; it sparkled like a crystallized jewel. Then she looked up at the summit. The storm clouds out of the sheer wall of the West Buttress meant more cold, stormy weather. It could last for days. How could they climb through this mess? No, she wouldn't think those thoughts any longer. Remember the monarch butterfly and its bright side. Somehow they would do it.

Sarah felt her face and head, the cheekbones still there, her hair balled up under her blue cap. It had been too long now since she'd been clean, but it didn't matter. Nothing mattered but climbing.

The worst was over, she tried to tell herself. She could stand anything. No, no, Sarah knew better than to think that. After Bobby's accident she had told herself that helping him had been her final big test. And then Sam had left. It couldn't get worse than that. And now after yesterday, she knew that there would be another test and another test, until finally she reached the summit or had to turn around. All she could do was take one step at a time until she could go no farther.

Ms. Harris had talked about how the snake was such a symbol of power in mythology. The snake always survived, shedding its skin and moving onward. Last night Sarah thought she saw her old skin roll out the door and tumble down the mountain.

Laura came out of the other tent and waved at Sarah. Walking slowly, Sarah went over to the kitchen area to meet her. Doug had talked so much of the difficulty they might have adjusting to the lower oxygen content of air at this altitude. "Remember folks, that if you're having trouble breathing, your mind's having trouble thinking too." Breathing was harder, no question about that.

"Good morning," Sarah said, putting on her best smile.

"Hi. I hear we both had bad days yesterday."

Sarah nodded, then stopped. "How is your altitude sickness?" All she'd been doing was thinking about herself.

"You know, now I don't think it was altitude sickness because I'm fine. It's just that I started my period and my body's all out of whack. It's a terrible time for it to come, but at least it's not something worse."

Sarah hugged Laura and said, "Well, I have no idea what I would do if it were me, but I'm so glad you're better. Because I just know Doug is going to get here today, and tomorrow it's summit, here we come."

"I hope so. I never thought I'd say this, but I miss him." They both laughed and started to get out the breakfast supplies.

"Laura, have you ever thought of getting married?" Sarah said, as she poured water into the pot and Laura started the stove.

"I almost was—once. A long time ago. We were very happy until . . ."

"He met somebody else?"

"He was killed."

Sarah almost dropped the pot. "I'm . . . I'm sorry. I had no idea."

"In a climbing accident."

"Oh God," Sarah said, looking off toward the summit.

"Not Denali. We talked about climbing it together. Jim died on Mount Foraker of pulmonary edema."

"Like Ray Genet?"

"Like Ray Genet."

Sarah stood for a moment, trying to absorb all that she was hearing. Then it dawned on her. "Mount Foraker," she said, pointing down and across the mountains. "It's that peak . . ."

"Right over there. I know. I think of Jim every time I look that way."

"But how can you— Wait a minute. The night that they called it McKinley's Woman and everybody started clapping and cheering . . ."

"It was hard. But in a way it was good. It kind of demystified it all, put it to rest." Laura put her arm around Sarah. "You wonder why I came?" Sarah nodded. "I had to come. After all these years of wondering, I had to find out why Jim loved to climb so much." Laura looked around and motioned with her hands. "And now I know. This—and," pointing to her heart, "this."

As they prepared the eggs, Laura kept talking, as if she were finally glad to tell Sarah the whole story. "Wendy got me to come, you know. We've taught together for over ten years, and during that time we've camped and hiked together many times. I would keep talking about mountain climbing and backing out of relationships with men. So finally last January she gave me a Summit Expeditions brochure and said, 'I think you're ready to do this. And I'd like to come along.'" Laura served up the eggs and handed Sarah a plate. "So we started training together and here we are."

Gabe, Wendy, and Sarah's dad showed up at about the same time. "Good morning," Laura said, handing them plates. Sarah kept looking at Laura. How little we really know about each other, she thought.

It seemed empty with just the five of them. They huddled together at breakfast, then afterward her dad suggested another marathon hearts game in the tent. Everybody nodded, including Gabe. "Count me out," Sarah said. She didn't want to waste her energy counting cards. She really wanted to be alone to write in her journal and prepare for the summit.

Sarah could feel her dad's eyes on her, begging her to play. "I'm all right, really," she said, giving everybody her biggest smile. "I'll come over later."

Back in the tent, Sarah pulled out the journal that had become such a companion to her.

Eighteen days on the mountain. I've almost made it, but still the biggest battle is in my head.

Sarah put down her pen and thought about Ms. Harris and how she never encouraged them to write blah, blah, blah entries. "Try to get below the surface stuff, class," she would always say.

Ms. Harris used to suggest things, like writing another person's view of an argument or problem. Had Sarah ever tried to write from her dad's point of view? No, it was too hard. Yet she could almost feel Ms. Harris's presence now, encouraging her to do so. Sarah had never tried the dialogue technique. It seemed too forced. But now she thought, if I try it, I can write from both our perspectives.

Sarah: You always seem to be on my case. Nothing I do is ever good enough.
Dad: That's not true. I think you're terrific.

Sarah: But you never told me that until yesterday when I almost had a nervous breakdown. Why couldn't you have told me earlier?

Dad: I thought you knew. I thought including you on this expedition expressed my feelings more than words ever could.

Sarah: Then why do you remind me about how many mistakes I'm making or how much money it's costing?

Dad: Because I have a hard time with money. I'm not making as much commission as I used to and I'm working twice as hard. Sometimes I feel like Willy Loman and the best years of my life are over.

Sarah: You're nothing like Willy Loman. You're only forty and handsome and funny. Willy was old and petty and trying to live his life through his kids.

Dad: How come you never told me that before? When I yell at you, I'm really yelling at myself. I hate my job, you know. I should have been a climbing guide instead of working for that damn company. I should have started my own company. I should have made the Olympic team in the 5,000 meter.

Sarah: I didn't know you ever worried about money. You're always so confident. And you were an incredible athlete, an NCAA All-American.

Dad: Weren't you upset when you didn't win as often last year as you did in middle school?

Sarah: But you got to compete in college on the national level. And I'm stuck in an Eskimo village that doesn't even have any running races. You won't even try to figure out a way for me to live with you.

Dad: I have no patience. If you lived with me, I'd probably yell at you all the time. You know me. I yell at myself. I yell at everybody. And now I spend half my life on the road.

Sarah: If you were home more, would you like me to live with you?

Dad: I think I would, but it scares me.

Sarah: It wouldn't be like being married to me.

Dad: Sarah, your mother's the one who finally divorced me.

Sarah: Because you practically deserted us. You were never around for days and weeks on end.

Dad: It's too complicated to explain, Sarah. I don't even understand it all myself.

Sarah: I don't want to tie you down, Dad. I just want to be with you before I'm grown up.

Sarah closed her journal and thought about her dad. If she was Artemis, who was he? Was he like the sun god Apollo, who stayed emotionally distant, yet always did the right thing? No, her dad was more like Poseidon, the god of the sea, with so many feelings buried underneath the surface. On the other hand, he was also like Ares, the emotional god of war, who always had to be embroiled in battle.

After lunch Sarah walked around the basin with Gabe. "Does it hurt your feelings that I don't like living in Mayurvik?"

"No. I didn't really like high school in Anchorage."

"You went to school in Anchorage? I didn't know that."

"There are so many things you don't know about me."

Sarah blushed. "You're right. There are many things I don't know about you, about Laura, even about my dad."

"I went to East Anchorage High the last two years of high school."

"And you hated it?"

"I didn't say that." Gabe paused and looked around. "There were many prejudiced people, but there were also some friendly students and teachers. There weren't many Native students." Gabe walked quickly and Sarah strained to hear his words. "I missed the hunting and fishing and my family, of course. And the Kass'aq food was so different."

"You lived with a white family?"

Gabe nodded. "So much talking. So much busyness But I got along. I adjusted. Some of my friends didn't. They dropped out and went home. I didn't blame them. Many times I wished I'd done the same."

"But how *did* you get along?"

"I went to school, even though it was hard at first, coming from my small village of three hundred people to a high school with two thousand students. I got used to being alone. I studied and did all right, even though many things were confusing for me. And I found a couple of teachers who seemed to like Natives, and they helped me out."

Sarah stopped and grabbed Gabe's arm. "But living with a white family, wasn't it hard? Why did you stay? Didn't your family miss you?"

"So many questions. Because I wanted to live and go to school in a city, so I would be ready for college. I wanted to find out how to make it in the Kass'aq world, so I could help my people."

"You have."

Gabe started walking again. "I don't know about that, but I did learn how to get along in another culture. Maybe not always like it, but at least how to get along in it, and not lose myself."

"I feel so foolish."

"What do you mean?"

"I've made such a mess of things in Mayurvik. I've had my mother and Mike, and you were all alone. And all I've done is complain about the long winters and having no friends because I was so different from everybody else."

"The people of Mayurvik might like your differences if you gave them a chance."

"But they don't talk very much."

"Well, I didn't talk very much at first, either, did I? Until I got to know and trust you." Gabe looked at Sarah. "You didn't talk so much in the beginning yourself. You Kass'aqs." He clicked his tongue. "Always rushing."

When they returned to the campsite, Doug was there, and Sarah greeted him with a squeal that floated through the swirling clouds.

"You can rest easy. Sam's just fine. He settled down the minute we got to 14,000 feet." Doug looked around at the group. "Have you all been resting? From the weather report, it sounds like tomorrow the weather might clear up here. If so, summit here we come!"

During the dinner of rice and beans, the wind picked up again. As they all sat eating, Laura said, "Look at the sky, will you?" Sarah turned and the sky was filled with shades of pink swirled in with the blue, just like her favorite Easter dress she had worn when she was seven. It seemed so long ago that she was an innocent child.

"Sleep well, folks. If the weather is the least bit cooperative, we are going for it. We've got to grab it when we can."

chapter 18

SOMETHING was different. An eerie silence surrounded the tent as Sarah tried to open her eyes. It was as if they were glued shut, and nothing could unstick them. Prying them open at last, she sat up, listening—no wind.

Clawing at the zipper on the tent door, Sarah finally got it open. She poked her head out and looked around, not caring how cold her ears got. She had to know if it was clear. Yes! Not a cloud in the sky. She waved at Doug over in the kitchen area, and he gave her the thumbs-up sign.

Pulling her head back into the tent, Sarah leaned over and shook her dad. "Dad. Dad. Wake up." Then she stopped, taking in short gasps of air. "This is it . . . This . . . is . . . Summit . . . Day."

John Janson grabbed his daughter's arm, and Sarah tried to slow down, to take deep breaths. She was at 17,000 feet, almost to the summit of Denali, and the excitement was so great Sarah thought the blood in her head might blow it wide open. She lay back down, dizzy, fearing she might faint if she stood up. Sarah knew she would need every ounce of strength to make it to the top today, but she couldn't slow down. She sat up again.

"Come on . . . Dad. We gotta . . . go. It's clear . . . outside. No . . . wind. Did you . . . hear me, no wind?" Her father started to dress. "And there's barely any snow on the ground. All the wind must have blown . . . it away during . . . the night, but we're going . . . to try for the summit, anyway. And we're . . . going to make it . . . I just know we're going to make the . . . summit."

She started talking faster again as she dressed. "We haven't a . . . moment to lose. The weather could change at any minute." Sarah felt as though she were shouting, but instead her words were coming out in spurts, shallow gasps that burst out, then faded away like the burps her cousin Tom used to make at holiday dinners to irritate his and Sarah's mothers.

Sarah wished her mother could be with them. They could have been the first mother-and-daughter team to climb Denali. Right now she was probably driving herself and Mike crazy in Fairbanks, worrying about Sarah every minute of the day.

"Sarah. Slow . . . down. Save your energy."

Sarah crawled out of the tent on her knees and stood looking at the mountain, trying to forget past mistakes. All the other days of climbing were only dress rehearsals for today.

She studied the blue black sky and noticed storm clouds forming in the east. She could see the winds blowing snow over the top of Denali, like stars around a queen's crown. How would they reach it in this weather? Her heart started pounding. No, she couldn't get nervous, not this early on. The weather could change four or five times before dinnertime. After almost three weeks on the mountain, she knew that by now.

If Doug said it was safe to go, it was safe. He'd been right so far. Besides, all they needed was five minutes, just five minutes to stand on the summit and hug the world. Five minutes—the time it took to move between geometry and biology at South Eugene High.

It was bitterly cold again, fifteen below with the wind-chill making the air much colder. At breakfast it seemed to Sarah that all six of them were working on nervous energy, boiling water, stirring the eggs, and drinking the hot chocolate that poured through Sarah's veins like hot lava.

Everybody was breathing hard and smiling but not talking, not wanting to waste a precious drop of energy. They knew one another so well now, and how important this summit was to each of them and to the three left behind. Now Sarah realized that none of them could do it alone—something she hadn't realized that first day in Talkeetna.

The calm air was strange, as though they were all encased inside a bubble. She only wished it could float them to the summit. Suddenly Doug's voice broke through the bubble.

"One final reminder, hardy climbers. The altitude pressure today will be *half* that of sea level. It's going to get harder and harder . . . to breathe normally. Don't . . . get .. discouraged. Just remember you are capable of only half your usual physical strength, so don't push too hard and . . . don't try to talk." Doug cleared his throat. "Your judgment can be impaired sometimes, too, as all of you . . . have already proven."

169

He waited for the laugh. It never came. "Don't worry. You'll be laughing at all my jokes after our successful summit bid today." Finally, Sarah let herself smile.

"One final word. Summit Day is fifty percent physical . . . and fifty percent mental. You'll need every . . . bit of your reserves today, body and mind. When the going gets tough—remember that you have it somewhere down deep. You wouldn't have gotten this far . . . if you don't."

Six A.M. Day 19. Strong winds picked up as they began climbing. Sarah worked against them, pushing her body straight ahead. If she let up for a moment, the wind was so strong it would push her off the safe path marked by Gabe ahead of her.

They slowed almost to a crawl, climbing up Denali Pass. Every step was a struggle. No matter what Doug had said, up till now, Sarah believed deep down that when someone was this close to the summit, the momentum alone would carry that person. Sarah's body ached all over, begging to stop. But the dream of reaching the summit was such a part of her now that it was like the sweat pouring out of her pores.

It took three hours for the sun to begin warming her, and for her sore and tired body to find the rhythm of climbing. A short granola-bar break renewed her energy. Starting up again, they traversed the south side of the saucer-shaped slope, following its contour as it gradually wound around the southern side of the mountain. Finally, she could see the summit. Why couldn't they just climb straight up to the top and get it over with? Sarah laughed inside. She was thinking like the old Bobby and his plan on the first climbing day—the quickest way between two points and the surest way to disaster and failure.

The slope was so hardened by wind Sarah knew she

could slip at any moment. She was tired, and when she got tired, her attention began to drift. She felt the knot in her stomach tighten up, almost anchoring her to the spot. Doug was right. Just breathing was hard work—breathing, something she'd always taken for granted until this trip. So this was how emphysema sufferers feel, she thought, struggling for every breath.

As they passed By Archdeacon's Tower, Sarah raised her eyes upward and prayed for the safety of all those present and for Sam, Tim, and Bobby. There was only a Catholic church in Mayurvik, and Sarah and her mom were Methodist, but they went to the Catholic mass sometimes. Sarah's belief in a higher being had strengthened on this trip. There had to be a reason for all this beauty and order in the universe.

Her dad looked so confident on the rope team ahead of theirs, so sure of his footing, so strong with his long legs and muscular arms. Like a bull he pushed up the mountain. Sarah wondered if her dad ever thought of God. He never used to go to church with them.

Right past Archdeacon's Tower they stopped for another break of Tang and dried fruit and crackers. Sarah forced herself to eat although she wasn't hungry. Doug said they should eat a lot today because of the cold and added strain. Sarah realized Doug had them stopping more often, as though they were out for a casual Sunday hike with plenty of time. Right, a Sunday hike during which you could hardly breathe.

All the days leading up to 14, Doug had pushed them hard. But after that he had taken it slower. Now, despite two rest days, Sarah knew she wasn't at her fighting strength, that her edge was off. Her legs and hips were stiff and her arms seemed to resist every planting of the ice ax.

She tried to summon the strength that had gotten her

through the earlier days. But all she could dream of were the warm shower and pizza waiting for her in Talkeetna. Her mind vacillated between sunbathing on a hot California beach and reaching the summit.

They continued up the mountain, seeing the orange wands that marked the western route to the summit. At least Doug didn't need the wands today to follow the route, Sarah thought, as he and Tim had so many other days. Sarah wished Tim could be with them. She knew that he would be proud of her.

Today couldn't have been clearer. Like a bug close to the ground, she could see every ridge in the snow, every cleat mark left by another climber's crampon, every tiny cloud in the crystal blue sky.

In her dreams Sarah had visualized this day to be like floating upward to an ice castle in the sky. Up ahead, Gabe did look as if he were floating, but Sarah felt that she was being pulled down to the center of the earth by a tremendous magnet.

She was so tired, she couldn't fight her fatigue anymore. She was more tired than she had ever been in her life, even when she had mononucleosis three years ago and had to stay in bed for three weeks. More tired than mile twenty-two of the marathon, when she hit the wall and had to get in the car with her dad.

Sarah tried to concentrate her eyes on the summit. She had missed seeing it since base camp. But now here it was, right there, jutting out of the sky like a rounded mound of white chocolate. All the other surrounding mountains looked like crystallized scoops of vanilla ice cream.

One step closer. Sarah kept hoping her muscles would miraculously have a surge of new energy, but no luck. Desperate, she felt around in her jacket pocket for a chocolate bar.

She wanted to sleep. She couldn't. She wanted to scream. No sound came out. At 14, Sarah had met a climber who talked about his mantra. She liked doing meditation, and had thought she would try using a mantra herself the next climbing day, but she had forgotten about it until now.

Clearing her mind of other thoughts, Sarah kept repeating. "To the summit, to the summit, to the summit." It helped her to relax as she moved slowly forward. "To the summit, to the summit."

But after what seemed like hours, Sarah didn't care if she ever made the summit—she just wanted to stop climbing. She tried concentrating on time, like a long-distance runner trying to clip off some fast miles. Five more minutes, just five more minutes. What was five more minutes in the rest of her life? Even without her watch, she still remembered what five minutes felt like.

She was cold, like the time when she was a little girl and had been ice-skating outdoors in Spokane with her cousins and got so cold she couldn't feel her toes and cried all the way home to her auntie's house. But this went even deeper. This was a cold in her heart, a feeling that she might never be warm again.

Sarah had read about Vern Tejas, the Denali guide who made the first solo winter ascent of Denali. One reporter had asked him, "How did you stay warm?"

"Warm? Hell, I was cold the whole time." Vern, Sarah thought, I'm with you.

Then it got even colder as the sun hid behind Denali. The wind was blowing as if it wanted to destroy every living thing on the mountain. Everywhere Sarah looked there was white—windblown white, not the glistening white of new snow, but the dull, flat white that creeps into your soul and leaves it frozen.

No trees, no flowers, just ridges of snow going on

forever. The only spot of color was her dad's bright red parka flashing out across the snow, like a stop sign ahead, warning all those who came near. At lunch Sarah was going to rip that red coat off her dad and put it on, running down the mountain. She didn't care if she lived, as long as she died in that red coat—in control, the source of all power.

Tim always said that everything above 14,000 feet was icing on the cake. Sarah had made it to 19,000 feet. Forget the summit, she thought. But what could she do? Lie down in the middle of this white world and cash it in?

Food. That was what she needed. Food. Not something white like vanilla ice cream or Swiss cheese or bread, but something red like apples or spaghetti with tomato sauce or a juicy steak. She needed food with real color, not those freeze-dried meals that looked like they had a half-life. That's what she had right now, a half-life, just putting one foot ahead of the other.

Sarah tried to focus her eyes, but everything became a blur. She kept looking for the football field. It should be straight ahead. Just when she thought she couldn't take another step, that each step would shove her through the soft snow and down to the bottom of the earth, she somehow found the strength to take another one.

It took five hours to climb to the edge of the football field at 19,200 feet. Finally, it lay right ahead, but where were the goal-posts? She couldn't hear the crowds cheering. She had to hear the cheering. Her heart felt as if it were covered with Visqueen, sweating, desperate to be released. Sarah would die to be a cheerleader right now, warm and sexy, cheering for South Eugene High School in a night game at Autzen Stadium, instead of climbing through this mess.

Sarah heard a laugh, a crazy woman's laugh, as though nothing mattered anymore. She had never wanted to be a cheerleader down on the field, with everybody watching every move she made. But, oh, how wonderful and safe that seemed right now. Let the guys in their pads sweat it out instead of her.

The flat stretch of snow called the football field looked as if it went on forever. Sarah started laughing again, silly little maniacal gulps. This was supposed to be a landmark? She shook her head. Only more of the same gruesome acres of flat snow.

No, she could do it. She used to run wind sprints in track practice. This would be like intervals. No, it was like the real thing. A race for the championship.

Doug called out, strong and tough. "Let's stop . . . for . . . lunch, gang. We need . . . a break . . . before the game." But even Doug's voice sounded slower.

Everyone gathered as if moving in slow motion. Sarah stood apart, woozy as if she were going to faint, colors of red, green, and blue washing across her brain. Laura came up and put her arm around her, guiding her to the group. They were all sitting on their packs, eating and talking slowly in short bursts, but their talk still had a lilt, whereas Sarah's was flat.

She looked around at their faces, but couldn't distinguish anyone. Then she heard her dad's voice. "Let's take off your pack." He put her pack on the ground and sat her down, handing her a water bottle. "Here, Sarah, drink this."

Sarah shook her head.

"Go . . . ahead. You need to take in more fluids."

"No . . . I . . . just want . . . to lie . . . back for a minute."

"No. There'll be . . . plenty of time for . . . that later. Today you've . . . still got a job to do."

Sarah shook her head again.

"Dad, I . . . don't . . . think I . . . can . . . make . . . it." She lay back against the snow and closed her eyes.

"Sarah, please. You are so strong. Your coach said you had the most efficient use of oxygen since Mary Decker Slaney. That's why you've done so well on this mountain, why you haven't been laid low by altitude sickness. Please, don't give up now."

Sarah felt so relaxed. It felt so good. Any moment her dad and Doug would be dragging her to her feet again, but for now she felt wonderful.

Suddenly she felt alone. Where was her dad? All Sarah could hear was the wind softly blowing around her and the faint echo of scattered voices.

A wave of fear overcame her. The voices had stopped. They had taken off without her. Sarah sat up quickly, the blood rushing to her head, and looked around. A few feet away, the rest of the group was quietly eating lunch. Her head throbbed as if her brains were knocking on her skull, begging to be set free.

Sarah had to get out of here. Wait. She could be free in an instant. All she had to do was unrope and start walking down the mountain.

Sarah stood up and started unfastening her harness. Gabe called out to her. Her dad came over and said, "Sarah, what are you doing? Please sit down. I'll bring you some lunch."

She stopped unfastening the harness and tried to concentrate on her dad's face and voice. She looked around. Where was she?

Then her mind cleared. She saw the faces of her friends and her dad, watching with concern. What was she thinking? Was she going to unrope and descend into possible death or sit here and refuse to go on, making her dad or Doug lose out while the others took the summit?

Gabe came over and said, "Sarah, *ingrim kangranun. Ingrim kangranun.* Repeat after me."

Together they said, *"Ingrim kangranun."*

"To the summit, Sarah. To the summit." Yes, she had to go on. She had to make the summit.

chapter 19

DOUG motioned the group to rope in for their journey across the football field. Then he walked over to Sarah and gave her a hug. Sarah looked down the field. Only two hundred feet of flat terrain. She'd run this distance thousands of times before in track practice. Her energy renewed, she thought this would be a cinch. But with her first step, she sank up to her knees in soft powder snow.

After sweating through the first few steps, Sarah looked up. The weather had changed dramatically around the summit. For the first time since base camp, she could actually see all of Denali, the summit in clear view, 700 feet above them. Like a huge monolith of rugged marble, it dominated the sky.

Sarah knew that some tourists stay in Denali National Park for weeks in the summer, hoping for a glimpse of the mountain. Now she understood why.

Tiny figures dotted the peak. They looked like ants

dragging food to their winter hideaway. Doug sent word back from the radio that a party was on the summit. Sarah narrowed her eyes and concentrated hard. She almost thought she could see them waving their arms in celebration.

Sarah's heart began beating faster. She was part of the mountain and, therefore, part of that expedition's celebration. Soon it would be her celebration. Struggling along, step by step, Sarah started visualizing what it was going to be like when she finally planted her marker and shouted her name. A circuit of energy charged through her body. She could make it now. In only a couple of hours she'd be on top of the world.

Sarah took another step and tried not to groan as she felt the powder snow seep into her wool socks. It was getting warmer now and she no longer felt so cold, but she still found it harder and harder to take a simple breath. Just drawing in air took so much energy. Up ahead of her on the rope, Sarah focused on Gabe's bright blue coat.

Gabe, Sarah, and Wendy started gaining on the other rope team. Then they were almost on top of Doug, her dad, and Laura. What was going on?

Finally, when they were right behind them, Gabe pulled around, so that the two teams were climbing side by side. Just as Sarah pulled up right across from her dad, he slumped to the ground, curled over, like an injured bear. Gabe stopped the team and Sarah knelt down and shook her dad. Not moving, with his eyes closed, he didn't even moan or cry out. Sarah felt his chest. he was breathing.

"Dad . . . Dad. Are . . . you all . . . right?" Sarah leaned over and tried to help her father up, but he didn't move.

"Come on . . . Dad. Let me help you up." Doug and Gabe stood nearby, but Sarah waved them away.

"Can't . . . tired . . . dizzy . . . my head hurts . . . leave . . . me . . . here." His voice so weak it came out in gasps.

"Come on . . . Dad. You can . . . do . . . it." Sarah had to stop to get her breath. "We're almost . . . to the . . . summit." Her father stared at Sarah, his eyes glazed.

"I'm . . . too . . . tired . . . to . . . fight." Sarah had never seen her dad like this before. She leaned over, and once again tried to get him up, but he was too heavy.

"Dad, you're . . . the one . . . who taught me . . . how." Sarah knew they had to stop talking and start moving again. Every word was taking up valuable energy and she felt her own fatigue coming back.

"Sarah, deep . . . down . . . I always . . . knew you . . . were better, could beat me . . . at . . ."

Sarah spit the words out, too angry to save her energy. "You're never going to understand, are you? I don't want to beat you. I want to be your daughter, not one of your sports buddies. And this isn't some stupid competition. It's a team effort. I wanted to do something with you, not against you. Get up. You're going . . . to the summit . . . if I have to . . . carry you every step . . . of the way."

Her dad took a few more labored breaths and extended his arm out to her. Sarah put her arm around her father's shoulder and hefted him up, his weight so heavy she thought she would collapse.

"I . . . always . . . knew you . . . were . . . stronger. Maybe that's . . . what I'm . . . afraid of."

Sarah put her glove to his mouth and shook her head. "Save your strength."

Side by side, they slowly crossed the field. The others

also slowed down, keeping the ropes taut. Step for step, Sarah and her dad moved together. Sarah longed to climb ahead and get it over with. But then she would look at her dad, and see the exhaustion and pain steeped in his face and think of the times he had kept her going on this trip.

She was so tired. But he was even more tired. Sarah didn't know how much longer she could stay with him. If her dad's strength didn't return, neither of them would make the summit, and possibly none of the others either.

Sarah started chanting in her head. "One step for Dad, let him be strong. One step for Bobby, let him be all right. One step for Tim, for all his understanding." Her eyes watered when she came to Sam. "One step for Sam. Let him make the summit someday."

Finally, when Sarah thought she could go no farther, when she thought she'd throw up from the pain and exhaustion, and have to let her dad go, she spotted the goal line only a few yards ahead. As if by magic, her dad rose up beside her, poised to score the winning touchdown at the Oregon-Washington game. Sarah gently pushed her father away. Finishing the crossing, her dad smiled and flashed a victory sign, then collapsed in Doug's arms. They'd been on the football field for over an hour. The football field was finally traversed, the touchdown scored. All that stood in the way of victory was the extra point.

Soon her dad was hugging Sarah, a smile lighting up his face. Pulling his shoulders back, he looked ready for the next play, while Sarah's legs buckled under her.

Gabe came over and helped her take off her pack. No matter what she told her dad, Sarah knew that she did not have enough strength to get them both to the top. But it looked like her dad didn't need her now.

Sarah tried to get up again. She had to get the climb over with, before she lost her momentum.

Doug insisted that they all break a while longer. He handed Sarah a granola bar, then gently rubbed her shoulders. "You were outstanding, kid."

Sarah smiled. Doug, good old bossy Doug. She got up and stretched side to side and tried to eat gorp and drink some water.

As they started climbing again and tackled the head wall of Denali, which extended from 19,600 to 20,000 feet, the closed-circuit energy of the group pushed Sarah forward. But she wondered how her dad was doing up ahead. Would his energy hold?

A lenticular cloud hung just below the summit, and once again the top of the High One was shrouded in a mist. The temperature was dropping, and Sarah felt the mist start to invade the edges of her mind, but not enough to overpower her growing excitement. As she climbed up the summit ridge at 20,000 feet, the top seemed so close she felt as if she could reach out and grab it with her hand.

The final 320-foot climb would take them up and over a little hill. Sarah could almost hear the orchestra swell. Everything was white and blurry. She stood at the bottom and wanted to sprint up, knees digging into the hill, lungs pumping, until she reached the top. But her body wouldn't cooperate. With every breath, she placed one foot in front of the other, and then started crawling, her eyes glued to the summit.

Sarah had dreamed about how easy these last few steps would be. But after nineteen days of climbing, she found the last steps as hard as the first ones almost three weeks before and the relief at reaching the top almost a letdown.

Until . . . until she looked out on all of North

America, the mountains and valleys, crevasses and avalanches, and down the mountain 14,000 feet—the most amazing sight Sarah had ever seen.

Together, the six of them stood and raised their arms. Tears swelled in Sarah's eyes. So this was the top of God's world. Bradford Washburn, the famous McKinley climber, had said it was a spiritual high, that you could see forever, or at least 100,000 miles. Washburn was right, thought Sarah. You could see forever.

Sarah squinted her eyes and thought she could make out the people of Talkeetna bustling around, preparing other climbers for their climb up Denali. Then she laughed, remembering Tim's story of the climbers who had mooned the small plane flying over the summit. Shivering, she thought, I wouldn't try that, not *this* trip, anyway.

She looked north toward Fairbanks and tried to shout, "Mom, I made it. I made it! I made it!" Only beeps of sound spurted out. But Sarah knew her mom was listening.

"Okay, everybody." With his big smile, Doug seemed like a new man. "To make it official . . . you really need to climb 150 feet . . . up to the top of the little hill." Doug stopped and took a breath. "That's what they claim . . . is the *real* summit. But be careful . . . You could get blown to . . . smithereens up there." Sarah strained to make out his words in the wind.

Gabe pushed Sarah on her way, and then her dad was by her side, grabbing her arm as they ascended the little hill, their heads bowed in the raging wind. On top they clutched each other and hugged, while Gabe took a photo from below. "Thank you, Dad. Oh, thank you, Dad."

"Thank you, Sarah." Sarah's dad grabbed her hand and they hurried back down to safer ground.

Day 19—4:30 P.M. They'd been climbing for ten and a half hours. They all kept hugging one another as if afraid to let go. All the cross words and close calls were forgotten. They'd made it as a team, on the collective strength of nine individuals working together. Sarah hugged Gabe. "Thanks. You really kept me going back at 17."

"Take your photos, June Bugs. We haven't got much time. It's late and cold." But Sarah didn't feel the cold. She felt as if she could stay on this mountain forever. It had touched something deep in her, a place she'd never been before, and she needed more than just a few moments to celebrate this feeling.

Laura read a poem she'd written for Jim. Doug planted three sticks in honor of his wife and two children. "I'll remove them and replant them next trip," he said. "I figure that guarantees I'll keep coming back." Sarah wondered why he'd never mentioned his family before. Or had she not been listening?

Months ago in Mayurvik, Sarah had debated what to leave on the summit. All she kept remembering were Tim's words, "Take only pictures, leave only footsteps." Pictures and memories were enough for Sarah. She and her dad took turns with the camera, taking as many shots as possible of the whole vista, hoping the camera was working. Then Sarah remembered that they had to do something in honor of Sam, Tim, and Bobby.

She gathered the group together. They sang one bar of "When Irish Eyes Are Smiling" for Sam. Then Wendy did an imitation of Bobby. "See. I told you I'd beat all you guys to the summit." Finally, for Tim, they all raised their arms and gave another cheer.

As they happily wrapped their arms around one another, Sarah wondered if they could keep these feelings going in the real world, away from the mountain.

Just when Sarah thought the surprises were over, Doug pulled out the shortwave radio and patched into a radio phone in Anchorage. He handed the radio to Sarah and said, "Here. Give the operator your mother's number and she'll make the call for you." Sarah's voice was shaking as she spoke to the operator and gave her the Fairbanks number her mother had made her memorize. Almost immediately she heard a ringing, but her body was quivering so much, she could hardly hang on to the radio.

"Hello . . . Hello . . . Mom, is that you? . . . It's me . . . Sarah. I'm calling from the . . . summit of Denali. I made it to the top . . ." Through her tears, Sarah tried to talk. "No, I'm . . . fine, Mom. I'm just . . . so . . . happy." By now the tears were running down her face and she handed the phone to her dad.

"Marlene, you'd really be proud of our daughter. She was something else today . . . Yes, we did. We really did it."

Sarah moved away by herself while the others made their phone calls. Soon she would be off this summit and she might lose this incredible feeling. She had to figure out a way to bottle up this exhilaration, this belief in herself. It was such heady stuff. Right now she felt that she could take on the world. Yes, she could. Tim told her long ago that Denali leaves a little part of itself with every climber who faces the mountain's challenges—a little part that would stay with her for the rest of her life. Nobody could take this experience away from her or tell her she didn't know how to persevere. Sarah felt the tears fill her eyes again, but it was too cold to cry. She'd just cry in her heart instead.

Doug gave one last call to make their final farewells

and prepare for the descent. Sarah remembered last night's dream. She was in heaven and looked down to see her and her dad standing at the summit, waving their arms in celebration. And now that's just the way it had happened. Sarah turned to join the others and found her dad waiting.

"Thanks for keeping me going today." He swept his arms around his daughter. "You made this possible for me."

"Stop it, Dad, *you* pushed me every step. We did it, Dad."

"Together."

Sarah hugged her dad. "I love you." She hadn't said that since the divorce.

"I love you too, Sarah."

chapter 20

ROPING in, Sarah kept looking around. She couldn't let the summit go so soon. But Doug hurried them along. "Folks, I know you are ecstatic . . . and so am I . . . But some of the most . . . tragic . . . accidents have happened after the summit, during the descent. Climbers get careless . . . thinking all the hard work is over. And you're tired. You've worked so hard. So just take your time and keep thinking . . . As they say, it's not over until the fat lady sings—or until we're safely back in Talkeetna."

They climbed quickly down to the football field, where it was safer to stop. Sarah hadn't realized how starving she was. She kept eating and eating—dried fruit, cheese, granola bars—anything she could get in her mouth. And nobody told her to slow down. Not her dad. Not Doug. Everyone was too busy eating.

The wind had stopped blowing, and Sarah felt relaxed in a way that she hadn't in months. She noticed Wendy and Doug talking quietly. Turning to Laura, she whispered, "It looks like Wendy and Doug are calling a truce."

Laura smiled. "Doug's got to admit that Wendy turned out to be a trooper. All of us were and you—pulling your dad across the football field."

Sarah shook her head. "It was more like just being there for him. But don't you just feel terrific? I'm so tired right now, I don't know how I did any of it today. But I did. We all did." Sarah looked over at her dad. "I'll bet he's embarrassed about the football field part."

"No, he's not. Didn't you hear him bragging to all of us about how you got him through the mighty defensive line?"

"I hope this changes things between us, Laura. It's really great right now because we're all so happy. But—"

Laura grabbed Sarah's arm. "Listen. Nobody can take away the experience you two have shared, all of us have shared. You can't help but know and trust each other better. You won't get along perfectly. But who ever does? You know, I think I'll prescribe a Denali climb to all my students and parents who are having problems. . . . And every husband and wife and friend and friend and . . ."

"Enemy and enemy and boss and employee." Sarah and Laura broke out laughing. "We should go into marketing for Summit Expeditions."

"Hey, what's so funny over there? Gabe and I are trying to have a serious conversation about photography."

"Well, we're not going to be serious anymore." And with that, Laura stuck her tongue out at Sarah's dad.

Sarah looked at her dad and at Laura and wondered . . . Wouldn't that be something?

Then she raised her voice. "Can you believe we made the summit? All that struggle and pain and frustration. Already I've forgotten that part, and all I remember is that glorious moment reaching the summit."

"That's what your mother said soon after you were born."

Sarah's eyes filled with tears. He did want her to be part of his life.

"Let's go, folks. Our sleeping bags are waiting at 17." Good old Doug. Always had to be the leader.

"Thanks, Laura," Sarah said as she walked by her friend to rope in.

"What for?"

"For being my friend and treating me like an adult."

"You are an adult, Sarah. I'm amazed at how sensitive and perceptive you are. And what drive! Some of my students could stand to be harder on themselves. But you. You need to take it easy." Laura tapped Sarah on the chest. "Life can't be serious all the time."

With the wind at her back and the pressure off, Sarah's body went into auto pilot. She was still being careful, but she felt as if she were floating. She enjoyed looking around, and taking in all the scenery she had been too worried to notice on the way up. Again, climbing through the football field was slow going, and she kept seeing a picture of her dad with his wounded eyes, but it was washed away by his grin on the summit.

It took four more hours to reach the camp at 17, but Sarah felt buoyed by the thrill of accomplishment. Studying the glaciers far below and watching the rivers move like tiny threads weaving through the land, she was carried along by the beauty. Better yet, her breathing got easier the closer she got to 17.

But not until Sarah reached the flat plateau at 17 did she realize how exhausted she truly was. Adrenalin had kept her pumped since the summit. But now she just wanted to sleep. Every muscle in her body ached, and she could hardly push herself to undress and roll into her sleeping bag. She looked over at her dad as he unrolled his sleeping bag. He looked like a battle-weary soldier too.

"Good night, Dad."

"Hey, listen to this," he said as he turned on the radio. "It's a burger commercial, a burger commercial at 17,000 feet. Should I ask if they deliver?"

"Sure thing. I'll take two cheeseburgers, a large fries, and a chocolate milkshake," Sarah said as she fell asleep, dreaming of the handsome French climbers who had also made the summit.

On Day 20 Sarah awoke rested and refreshed, anxious to get going. The call of hot showers, soda, ice cream, fresh fruit, salad, pizza, television, and a soft bed was getting louder and louder. At breakfast she looked around at the campsites filled with climbers, and silently wished good luck to those going up.

They broke camp at 9 A.M., taking time only to pack up the remaining supplies. Once again it was cold and windy, but it didn't seem so bad, now that Sarah was heading the other way. She wondered how strong she'd be if she were making an assault on the summit today, and then she shook her head. She had been strong when she needed to be. All she had to do now was safely get down the mountain, and afterward she could sleep for a month.

As they began climbing down, Sarah's body felt drained and physically weaker. She remembered that feeling from her post-marathon days. But her mind felt so free of worry and uncertainty and so much more joyful than after the marathon.

It took two hours to reach 16, where they dismantled the large cache that they had built to store the emergency supplies. Even though they had camouflaged it in the snow, the ravens had gotten into it. Doug was furious. "Those damn birds. They can't leave anything alone."

Sarah was so grateful they hadn't needed the supplies, that for all she cared the birds could have the food. But when she looked at Doug, she thought about how he must feel, trying to outfox the ravens several times a summer. Ever since reading Poe's poem "The Raven," Sarah thought the bird was romantic, until last year in Mayurvik when she watched the ravens scrounge around the dump.

Descending from 16 to 15, Sarah stopped at the bottom of the fixed line, unhooked her jumar, and then looked up. How much easier it was going down than struggling up that icy slope. She watched her dad daydreaming and wondered what he was thinking.

Next to Sarah, Wendy spoke, looking over at Gabe. "Gabe's a good man. What a help he's been on the trip. It's funny, though. Of all of us, he's said the least about making the summit."

"Sometimes it's different in other cultures, Wendy. Look how he's smiling. The Yup'iks use so many more nonverbal signals to express their feelings than we do. Some outsiders take the silence for ignorance, but I'd call it wisdom." Sarah took a deep breath and looked away. "You know, I wish I'd known Gabe in Mayurvik. Maybe I wouldn't have been so confused all year."

Wendy squeezed Sarah's arm. "But maybe that confusion has helped form your perceptions now. I know it has helped mine. I've always pretended to be the tough outdoorswoman, afraid to show weakness. But this trip I've learned I really am strong and can be myself around men, no matter what. Thanks. You've just taught me something."

At 2 P.M. they reached Genet Basin, hoping to find Bobby and Tim waiting for them. Instead, Sam came up and hugged Sarah from behind.

"Congratulations, kid. You did it."

"Sam, oh, Sam." Sarah hugged him back. "I didn't think you'd be here. Are you all right?"

"I'm fine. Really. The minute I arrived back here I was my old self in no time. Tell me. Was it as great as they say?"

"Oh, Sam. It was . . . but I wanted you to be with us so badly. You helped get me across the football field, though. The snow was so deep and it took so long and then Dad collapsed and I had to help him. I just kept saying, one step for Sam, one step for Sam."

Sam hugged her again and kissed her on both cheeks. "I knew I'd be there in spirit. Don't say any more. It's okay. It's okay," Sam said as both he and Sarah cried. "I'll be back. I'll be back, and next time I'll reach the summit. I just went as far as I could go. So I can't be down on myself. I gave it my best shot. Not half bad for a former two-pack-a-day smoker."

Sarah stopped crying and looked up at her friend. "But you know, Sam, the best part has been getting close to the people like you who have helped me so much."

Doug announced that he had radioed to Tim at 11 and that he and Bobby would be waiting for them when they arrived. So the group voted to eat a quick lunch and keep moving. As they traveled, Sarah kept an eye on Sam up ahead. Memories of his earlier collapse still played in her mind. But he only seemed to get livelier and livelier the farther down they climbed. His tunes wafted up to Sarah throughout the afternoon.

Coming into camp at 11, they were greeted by Bobby

and Tim with cheers and yells. Sarah was so happy to see them. Something had been missing. And now hugging and sharing stories at dinner, the circle was complete. Tim even announced that for dessert they would be having snow ice cream—snow with instant Jell-O mixed in—in honor of the reunion.

Sarah kept sneaking glances at Bobby. Finally, he came up to her. "Stop staring at me. I'm fine. I pulled the muscles in my upper arm and freaked out about the whole crevasse thing, but now I'm fine. So don't treat me like a broken egg or something."

Sarah laughed. "Well, thank God, the old Bobby is back, alive and well."

"You know, Sarah, I'm going to make that summit next year. No crevasse falls, no altitude sicknness, just up and over for me. I had the flu about a week before we left and I think it strung me out."

"Bobby. Shut up. I know you could have done it. And I know you will. Right now I just want you to know that it wasn't the same without you. I even missed your nonstop commentary." She smiled. "Well . . . at least part of the time."

After dinner Bobby and Sam wanted to know about every step of the trip between 17 and the summit. Everybody interrupted everybody else, trying to be the one to tell the most dramatic parts. Suddenly Bobby turned to Sarah and switched the conversation. "I'm jealous of you and your dad, Sarah. My dad left when I was three years old and I've never seen him since."

"I'm divorced, Bobby."

Sarah blinked her eyes open. How could she not know that about Sam after all this time? Who would want to divorce sweet Sam?

"But I'll bet you didn't desert your kids."

"Nope, but it hasn't been easy, trying to work out a

blended family. It was the only way though. I tried to talk my two sons into coming along with me, but they're both too busy with school or jobs."

Going to sleep later, Sarah thought about divorce. How so many kids and adults are touched by it nowadays. Then she pulled out her notebook and decided to write her mother that long overdue letter.

Dear Mom,

You've no idea how the quotes you wrote in the journal have kept me going. I made it to the top, Mom. I did it and I'm so proud of myself. Thank you for supporting me on this trip and all this year, especially now that I realize what a royal pain in the behind I was.

I just found your last quote, way at the back of the journal, which seems to say it all for me.

"If we are always arriving and departing,
it is also true that we are eternally anchored.
One's destination is never a place, but rather
a new way of looking at things."

—Henry Miller

Tim, the guide, said that I would never be the same again after climbing Denali. And right now I feel that's true. Climbing Denali is like something that becomes a part of you. I'm not sure what that means yet, but I absolutely love the feeling, and it's one of the things that has made me the happiest of anything I've done. It's like making the summit has touched a place in my heart, a place so deep, I didn't know it existed.

chapter 21

SARAH kept smiling and pinching herself the next day—Day 21—exactly three weeks on the mountain. The terrific feeling just stayed with her. Nothing bothered her. She'd been warned about a let-down, but it hadn't come yet.

The six-hour climb from 11 to 7 passed as on any day during the trip, except they were going down, their packs light with only garbage and extra supplies left to carry out. Early on, Tim had explained the National Park regulations about carrying out garbage. Sarah was disgusted to think that even people who climbed Denali left trash. How could you love the outdoors and at the same time leave trash and litter? she wondered. It didn't fit.

On this last day of climbing, Sarah tried to remember every moment of the trip, the good and the bad, but it all blended as if in a dream. Already she seemed to be losing parts of the experience—all but the good times:

the talks with Laura, jokes with Sam, photography lessons with Gabe, the incredible scenery, and the power of the ice ax and rope in her hand. And the time spent with her dad.

As slow as the snowshoes had seemed on the trip up the mountain, Sarah enjoyed wearing them again. She pretended she was an old sourdough trapper out hunting moose or bear for dinner. Her beard hung to her knees and she hadn't had a shower for months. Moving along, she smiled and thought, shower, shower, shower. Pizza, pizza, pizza.

In a few more hours she'd be clean, really clean. But then she'd have to start worrying about how she looked again. After a few days on Denali, all worries about appearance had flown away, especially when the reflection in her sunglasses was the only way for her to tell how she looked. Like giving up time, Sarah had loved giving up primping. Not that she'd ever been one to spend hours in the bathroom putting on layers of makeup. But she liked to look good. Who didn't?

As they all slogged up the over 300-foot Heartbreak Hill and down into Kahiltna base camp, Sarah was overwhelmed with sadness. The trip was almost over and she could never get it back.

Don, their pilot, was waiting with the ingredients for Summit's famous spaghetti dinner. Everyone was laughing and teasing, but Sarah couldn't relax. She had to keep these last twenty-one days wrapped tightly in her heart.

Sarah ate until she was about to burst, and then kept right on eating French bread as she watched the first planeload depart for Talkeetna. Later she kept herself busy fooling around with the equipment, so that she ended up on the last plane ride. She was determined to be the last one to leave.

Sarah and Tim finished up the cleanup. "So where's the happy climber of a few hours ago?" Tim asked.

"I don't want to let this trip go, Tim. It has meant so much to me. And now I'm afraid I'll leave here and go back to being the same old negative Sarah."

Tim stopped packing a box of food and stood up. "Whoa, there. Sarah, life is always better after you've climbed Denali. You already know that. Do you just need to hear it again? Once you've climbed Denali nothing can ever seem impossible again."

Too soon Don buzzed overhead, and Sarah found herself loaded up in the plane with her dad and Tim, waving farewell to her mountain. True to her promise, she was the last one to step off the ground of Kahiltna Glacier.

Winging back to Talkeetna, this time Sarah was far more concerned with the scenery than with her stomach. By eight o'clock everyone was safely back in Talkeetna eating again. After a round of showers, the guides had ordered pizzas, and everyone but Sarah was drinking beer. Tomorrow they would hold a formal debriefing, but tonight was for celebrating.

As she took her first bite of pepperoni pizza, her dad sat down. "Hey, you look pretty handsome, Dad. No more grungy hair."

Her dad tousled his hair and laughed. "I don't know. I kind of liked it that way. You know, the James Dean look." Then he stopped and lowered his voice. "Your mom and Mike will be here sometime tomorrow. Maybe you and I should talk about next year before they come." Sarah didn't say anything. "Or maybe all four of us could talk about it."

"I'd like that, Dad. And I know Mom would too." Then as if embarrassed, her dad looked away. "Dad?

Thanks. Thanks for everything." Just then Gabe and Laura joined their table.

"So Gabe, when's your next trip up Denali, you lucky dog," Sarah said, drinking her orange juice. Gabe smiled and took a piece of pizza.

"Next week. I'll spend a couple of days helping out in the Anchorage office first and sleeping a lot too. How about you?"

"I'm going back to Fairbanks with my mom and stepdad for a few days and then spend some more time with my dad."

"And what about next year?"

"I don't know, Gabe. But I'm not as worried anymore. My dad just said he's ready to talk about it. It's funny, though, this climb and talking to you helped me realize how much I missed out on in Mayurvik. How I didn't take advantage of what was right in front of me."

"I didn't mean—"

"No, it wasn't what you said. It was you. How much you love your culture and how you've struggled living outside it, but survived, anyway. Gabe, I'm so glad you were on the trip."

"I'm glad you were on the trip, too, Sarah."

"You're a great guide, Gabe. I can see you doing it for a long time."

"I don't know. The corporation wants me back come September. My family misses me in Peñarmiut. But I'll figure it out sometime. So will you." They both smiled and grabbed for the same piece of pizza, then burst into laugher, playing tug-of-war.

Wendy yelled over. "Hey, what's all the ruckus about?"

"Yeah," piped in Doug.

"Wendy," Sarah yelled out. "You're the greatest!" Wendy stood up and everyone cheered for her, then

Doug stood up, then all of them, one by one, stood and were applauded. Sarah looked around at the nine of them. She loved these people, warts and all.

An hour into the madness, Sarah sneaked out the back door for a walk. Never much of a partier, she was having trouble getting used to the blaring radio, ringing telephone, and all the loud talking after the quiet of the mountain.

She walked out to the dirt airstrip, where she had stood three weeks ago and looked up at Denali, wondering who was struggling on his journey up the summit tonight. She prayed that he might find his way.

I've been there, she thought. All the way to the top. Sarah's body felt warm, even though she wore no sweater and the night temperature was cool.

Tim came walking out toward her. "Mind if I join you? Our talk got interrupted earlier."

"No, there's so much more I want to tell you. Like how very much I wish you could have been with us at the summit. You more than anybody helped me believe, from the very beginning, that I could do it."

"But after a while you didn't need me, Sarah. You got stronger, you made friends, you started believing in yourself." Tim and Sarah turned around and began walking back down the airstrip.

"But I never would have come on this trip if you hadn't convinced me over the phone that I could do it. Here I'd already talked my dad into bringing me along and then I was about to chicken out on the greatest experience of my life. It was, Tim." Sarah stopped and grabbed Tim's arm. "It was so hard and so wonderful all at the same time." Tim nodded.

"I heard you really pulled your dad through at the end."

"I guess . . . No, I did, in a way. But he and Gàbe

really pulled me through a couple of days before when I had a mini-breakdown and wanted to run crazy down the mountain. I guess we all helped one another out . . . I hope this all makes a difference with my dad and me.''

"How can it not? Denali is bigger than all of us. Like I said before, there is no way a person isn't changed by climbing it. Well, I'll leave you to your thoughts." Tim turned toward the lodge.

"Tim?"

"Yeah?"

"Thanks. I hope I meet a guy like you when I'm older."

"You will." Then he laughed. "There are plenty of good men around. And if you meet one who isn't as good as he could be, and you're still in love with him anyway, send him on an expedition up Denali."

Yes, Denali would still be there in all its glory. It would always be there for Sarah to come back to. Sarah felt that all she'd done for the past three days was hug people. So now she wrapped her arms around her body and hugged herself. Then she walked back to the party.

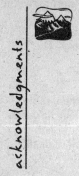

acknowledgments

SPECIAL thanks go to the Genet Expedition guides who willingly answered all my infinite questions about climbing Denali: Ken Blue, Mike Howerton, and Anne Morris. Also to climbers Cindy Folsom, Ken Green, Shannon Hoffman, and Brian Sweet; Yup'ik language consultants Andy and Hubert Angaiak and Walter Tirchik; and poet Alice Evans.

I would also like to thank Scot Christian and his seventh-grade English students at Bethel Regional High School in Bethel, Alaska, who read and responded to *To the Summit* as a work in progress, as did Carolyn Kremers, writer and outdoorswoman. And thanks to my editor, Virginia Buckley, for her patience and encouragement.

Finally love to my family—Murph, Conor, and Megan—for all their support.